Introduction to Virtue Ethics

Insights of the Ancient Greeks

RAYMOND J. DEVETTERE

Georgetown University Press / Washington, D.C.

Georgetown University Press, Washington, D.C.
© 2002 by Georgetown University Press. All rights reserved.
Printed in the United States of America

10 9 8 7 6 5 4 3 2 1   2002

This volume is printed on acid-free offset book paper.

Library of Congress Cataloging-in-Publication Data

Devettere, Raymond J.
  Introduction to virtue ethics : insights of the ancient Greeks / Raymond J.
Devettere.
      p. cm.
  Includes bibliographical references and index.
  ISBN 0-87840-372-8 (pbk : alk. paper)
      1. Ethics, Ancient. 2. Virute—History. 3. Prudence—History.
4. Ethics—Greece—History. I. Title.

BJ171.V55 D48 2002
170'.938—dc21   2002023630

For Paula

Contents

Introduction

This book is an introduction to the beginnings of virtue ethics. It takes the reader back to the Greeks—Socrates, Plato, Aristotle, Epicurus, and the early Stoics—and to the moral philosophy they created in the fourth and third centuries before the common era (B.C.E.). Reading the ancient Greek moral philosophers reminds us how much their fundamental ethical ideas differ from modern ideas. The seminal ethical notion today is that ethics is about obligations arising from moral laws or principles. Where these moral laws and principles come from, of course, is a matter of disagreement. For some, the source of moral obligation is still religious— God's law written as written in the sacred texts or inscribed in the human heart.

With the Enlightenment in the eighteenth century, the idea that moral obligation is grounded in God's laws and religion began losing its appeal for many. Here a philosopher named Immanuel Kant (1724–1804) represents a transitional figure. Despite being a devout Christian he nonetheless insisted that the moral law does not come from God but from ourselves. Thanks to what he called "pure practical reason," he thought that we can set forth a categorical imperative by which we generate maxims telling us what we ought and ought not to do—our duties—and our moral obligation is to act accordingly. Today, Kant's moral theory is called a deontological theory; that is, a theory that judges some actions as ethical or unethical in themselves, regardless of the agent's intentions and the situational circumstances.

Yet, Kant retained an important part of his Christian religious tradition by insisting that two beliefs—the belief in immortality and the belief in God—although not something that pure reason can establish, are necessary postulates of his moral theory. He thus preserved the traditional Christian motivation for being ethical: there is a life after death where a just God will provide happiness for those worthy of it. Today, few philosophers whose work is inspired by Kant's ethics retain those two postulates that he thought were so necessary for ethics. The result is that modern Kantian approaches to ethics provide us with impressive moral theories but not a good explanation why we ought to carry out the duties prescribed by the maxims and principles derived from a categorical imperative that we legislate for ourselves.

John Stuart Mill (1806–1873), one of utilitarianism's founding fathers, strenuously disagreed with Kant's approach. He argued that we do not derive our obligations from pure reason but from the actual consequences of our actions. Instead of deriving moral maxims and duties from a foundational categorical imperative, we derive them from the "principle of utility" or the "greatest happiness principle." According to the "principle of utility," we ought to follow whatever principles and rules are useful for achieving the greatest happiness for the greatest number. Utilitarian theories are thus moralities of obligation no less than deontological theories; they tell us that we are obliged to follow the principles and rules derived from the greatest happiness principle.

Unlike Kant, however, Mill did not insist that beliefs in immortality and a just God to provide happiness after death are necessary postulates of ethics. Thus, utilitarianism, no less than most contemporary versions of the Kantian approach, declines to insist on what was the most convincing traditional reason for fulfilling our moral obligations—the belief in immortality and God.

Modern ethics has inherited from religious traditions the idea that ethics is about obligations arising from moral laws and principles, yet it insists that the laws and principles producing the obligations do not come from religion. In place of a religious account of how we obtain our moral laws and principles, they offer a philosophical account. However, there is no agreement on which moral philosophy or theory should prevail—whole families of Kantian and utilitarian theories now exist. Moreover, other theories continue to surface; for example, the ethics of care; the revival of an ethics known as casuistry, which derives its principles from resolved cases; and the ethics of expressivism or projectivism, an approach with roots in the work of David Hume and Adam Smith that emphasizes feelings and sentiments.

None of these approaches has a good explanation of why we ought to follow the principles they propose. Why should anyone obey Kant's strict duties never to lie or break promises or commit suicide in the last stage of terminal illness once his "necessary postulate" of God judging people in a life after death has disappeared from Kantian ethics? Why should anyone feel obliged to follow the utilitarian principle of seeking the greatest happiness of the greatest number, or follow rules designed to accomplish this, whenever doing so will be at great cost to him or his loved ones? Why should I care for you if it will cost me? Why should I accept principles derived from previously settled cases to determine how I should live now? How can I trust my natural sentiments when I realize that human nature harbors instincts for death and destruction as well as for life, benevolence, and sympathy?

Modern moral philosophy is thus arguably in a state of disarray and distress. It retains the language of obligation arising from moral laws, principles, and rules but rejects the religious underpinnings that once provided both the source of the moral law and the motive for observing it. To overcome the disarray and distress, some suggest a return to a religious foundation for ethics. Others suggest that one of the modern theories of obligation will eventually triumph over its competitors. This book suggests a third option: we might learn something from the insights of the philosophers in ancient Greece who first developed virtue ethics.

In reading the ancient works of Greek ethics, we find a whole new world. Greek ethics is about happiness, not obligation or duty. It is about deliberation, not law. It is grounded in experience, not moral theory. And the motivation for being ethical comes from the deepest of human desires—the desire to make our lives go well.

The desire to flourish, to live a good life, and to find happiness while we live—this is what drives Greek ethics. Obligation simply is not a fundamental category because it makes no sense to say that we have an obligation to seek happiness when happiness is already what we most yearn for in our lives. What the Greeks call virtue is simply another name for what makes our lives good lives, that is, lives of happiness.

Getting to know the fundamental ideas of Greek virtue ethics is not easy. The primary manuscripts are not perfect, interpretations are difficult, translations can be misleading, and scholars disagree on many issues. Nonetheless, it is important both for those advocating virtue ethics and for those preferring other approaches to have some familiarity with the fundamental ideas behind the development of ancient virtue ethics.

This introduction avoids two common ways of retrieving ideas from ancient philosophy. One way is to claim that one is giving a new and definitive interpretation of the ancient philosophers, the other way is to say that one is simply adding another interpretation to the several interpretations that already exist. This book aims to sidestep both these approaches by encouraging the reader to read the ancient philosophers themselves. It invites the reader to set aside the preconception that ethics is about obligations arising from moral laws and principles, to bracket what is being said about virtue ethics in current treatments that make little reference to the ancient texts, and then to go back and see what is there in the writings of Plato, Aristotle, Epicurus, the Stoics, and others.

In going back to the ancient texts, the reader needs to be aware that there are many translations and they often use different words to translate the Greek terminology. This can be confusing and misleading for readers not familiar with ancient Greek. To avoid this pitfall and to ensure uniformity of language in this book, all the translations of Greek and Latin words and phrases are my own.

By reading the ancient works the reader will discover a new and challenging way to think about ethics. He or she will also discover how demanding is the task of understanding what the authors are saying. A reader will soon appreciate the outstanding work being done by scholars capable of reading ancient Greek and familiar with Greek philosophy. A sampling of some of the recent important work in ancient virtue ethics is found in the bibliographical essay at the end of this book. I owe much to these authors and encourage readers interested in virtue ethics to familiarize themselves not only with the primary sources but with the impressive scholarship on ancient virtue ethics that remains largely unknown outside the field of ancient philosophy.

By returning to the ancient texts and also by becoming aware of the work being done in ancient philosophy, the reader will realize that much of what passes for "virtue ethics" today is far different from what its founders had in mind. In ancient ethics, virtues such as justice and love, for example, do not tell us what we ought to do. And prudence or practical wisdom, the virtue that does tell us what to decide and do, is not about applying principles and rules with sensitivity and discretion, nor is it about knowing when to make exceptions to principles and rules, nor is it about resolving conflicts among principles and rules. Prudence precedes all moral laws, principles, and rules. Prudence is *the* moral norm both for personal decision making and for making any kind of rules regulating human behavior.

The vision of the ancient ethicists is the good life, a life well lived, happiness. They thought that developing a virtuous character was necessary (some say sufficient) for realizing this vision. And they thought that prudence (practical wisdom, practical reasoning) was the way to make the decisions that develop an authentic virtuous character. The following chapters will, I hope, show the reader what role character virtues such as justice and love play in ancient ethics and how the intellectual virtue known as prudence serves as the guide for making the ethical decisions that develop the authentic character virtues in our lives.

PART ONE

Desire, Happiness, and Virtue

What gives rise to the idea that some behaviors are good or right and other behaviors are bad or wrong? What, in other words, is the origin of what we call ethics or morality? The possible sources are many. Undoubtedly, some sources are cultural—social customs, the dictates of authority figures (patriarchs, tribal chiefs, kings, emperors, and so forth), as well as the codes and laws generated by advanced civilizations. Another source might be biological—evolutionary biology suggests moral behavior plays a role in the survival of the species. Still another source might be psychological—perhaps at least some of what we call morality arises from the cunning of the weak to tame the powerful, as Nietzsche claimed, or from the unconscious internalization of the rules needed to survive in civilization, as Freud claimed.

Although some or all of these factors probably play a role in the genesis of what we call ethics and morality, there is a long tradition that refuses to reduce morality to any one of them, or even to all of them. This moral tradition insists that there is something more to the origin of ethics than custom, dictates, laws, biology, and psychological drives or needs. Moralists have presented this "something more" in two ways: Some say the something more is religion, others say it is reason. Of course, those embracing a religious ethic often find a place for reason, and those embracing a rational ethic often find a place for religion.

The ancient peoples of the great empires in the Middle East—Babylonia is one important example—advocated a religious morality. Morality was something revealed by a deity and promulgated by the leader of the people. The picture carved at the top of the famous stone slab known as the Code of Hammurabi almost four thousand years ago shows a Babylonian god, either Marduk or Shamash, handing the moral code to Hammurabi, the king of Babylonia. And the first books of the Hebrew bible, written about three thousand years ago, describe Yahweh giving the Ten Commandments and other laws to Moses, the leader of the descendants of Abraham who was born and raised in Babylonia about the time of Hammurabi.

Twenty-four hundred years ago, the Greek philosophers turned not to religion but to reason for the "something more" in morality. Unlike Semitic peoples, who located the source of morality in divine revelation, the Greeks located it in human reasoning.

In fifth century Athens, Socrates began challenging some key Sophist doctrines. "Man is the measure of all things," the Sophist Protagoras is supposed to have said, suggesting that truth and value are relative. Not so, said Socrates. Knowledge of things as they truly are, and not what a person thinks they are, is what we need if we are to discover what makes life a success and how we can achieve it. Socrates and the Greek philosophers relied on human reason, not divine revelation, to learn what made a life truly good and to discern what actions are right and what actions are wrong. The Greek approach to morality thus differs significantly from that of the Middle East.

The tension between viewing ethics and morality as fundamentally religious or as fundamentally rational still runs deep in our culture. But it is not the only major tension. A second tension centers on whether we view morality primarily in terms of our obligations or primarily in terms of our desires for what is good. Middle Eastern religious moralities are moralities of obligation: the law and commandments have a divine origin and our obligation is to obey them. However, moralities of obligation need not be religious. Some Roman Stoics proposed a morality of obligation based on natural law. In modern times Kantians and utilitarians propose moralities of obligation and even the effort to develop a rights-based morality remains within the camp of obligation moralities—if I have a right to life your obligation is to respect it and if I have a right to choose your obligation is to respect that right.

Two fundamental tensions are thus entwined in our ethical tradition. One tension, the older one, is the conflict between moralities making religion and divine revelation fundamental and moralities making reason and human experience fundamental. The second tension is the conflict between moralities of obligation, which may or may not be religious, and moralities of the good. Moralities of obligation are known for the normative role they give to moral laws, principles, rules, and rights in decision making while moralities of the good are known for the normative role they give to the virtue of prudence in decision making.

The two conflicts obviously overlap somewhat. References to the gods are frequent in the virtue ethics of Socrates, Plato, Aristotle, and the Stoics, and the need for reason to interpret and apply divinely inspired laws is widely recognized, at least to some degree, in the religious traditions of Judaism and Christianity, as the rab-binical commentaries and rich tradition of moral theologies show so well. Also, many theories of obligation include a role for virtue while virtue ethics includes a place for obligations. However, when virtue ethics is understood the way the early Greeks understood it, moralities of virtue and moralities of obliga-tion are ultimately incompatible. Early virtue-based ethics insists that the good is fundamental and not obligation—it makes no sense to think we are obliged to pursue the good because it is what we desire anyway. Rule-based ethics, on the other hand, insists that obligation is fundamental—moral laws, principles, rules, and rights impose on us certain obligations. Virtue theories view moral agents as people freely pursuing their desire for happiness in life while ob-ligation theories see moral agents as people subject to some kind of moral principles that are either revealed by a deity or derived from a moral theory.

The two approaches have different foundations. If you drive a rule-based approach back to its foundation with questions such as where do the rule-like commandments or principles creating the obligations come from, then you ultimately arrive at either a law-giving God or a principle-generating philosophical theory. Any ethics that makes obligation fundamental inevitably has to give an account of who or what generates the moral laws or moral principles creating the obligations. A theology that conceives of God as a legislator giving commandments offers one such account of obligation but it is not the only one. Moral philosophy proposes a number of other accounts; namely, the powerful theories that de-rive obligations from moral principles derived from accounts of human nature (natural law theories), or from ideas about natural rights (rights-based theories), or from a critical analysis of "pure" reason (Kantian theories), or from a consideration of conse-quences (utilitarianism), or from a history of analogous cases (casuistry).

On the other hand, if you drive the virtue-based approach of the Greeks back to its foundation, you will not arrive at a deity or a theory. You will arrive at nothing more than human experience. Virtue ethics is not rooted in religious revelation or in moral the-ory but in an examination of human experience. The virtue ethicist can only ask each person, as Socrates did, to think critically about his or her life and how best to live it. What gives virtue ethics its appeal for some people—and what makes it so unacceptable for others—is the fact that its foundation is not a deity or a theory but a carefully examined life.

The foundation of ancient virtue ethics lies in a personal examination of human experience, the effort of each person to examine his or her life and ask how it is going. "The unexamined life is not worth living" is perhaps the best known quote attributed to Socrates, and so we begin our introduction to virtue ethics by looking at the Socrates we find asking questions in Plato's *Apology* and in some early Platonic dialogues. Here, we discover him examining his life and discovering how best to live it.

CHAPTER 1

The Origin of Ethics

Desires and Impulses

What kind of life is worth living? wonders Socrates. The question implies two things: first, not all kinds of life are worth living and, second, one kind of life not worth living is the unexamined life. Ethics begins when we examine our lives and ask: How should we be living and what should we be doing?

We can answer these questions well only if we know what we want most from life. We know that we want more from life than life itself. We want good things in life, and we want to live well and to do well. We want what the Stoics call a "good flow" in life. Human life is a life of longing and desire for a good life.

Virtue ethics is rooted in this desire. By "desire" we mean something stronger than a mere wish such as "I wish I had something to drink" or "I wish I were rich." Mere wishes remain wishful thinking; they do not initiate behavior. By desire, on the other hand, we mean that which actually initiates behaviors—the actions aimed at achieving whatever is desired. My desires for something to drink or for wealth, unlike mere wishes, will actually generate behaviors aimed at getting something to drink or becoming wealthy.

Desires are the wellsprings of the activities that constitute human living. If ethics is about our life-forming activities, about what we do, and if what we do originates in our natural desires, then ethics originates in our natural desires for doing well and living well.

Because desires are the wellspring of living and doing, it is not surprising that the early ethicists developed extensive psychological accounts of human desires.

Their accounts of desire vary somewhat, as we would expect, and we need to explore the important variations because they affect the way that different philosophers understand the virtues. A major disagreement in the ancient accounts of the psychology of desire springs from the distinction between rational and nonrational desires. Rational desires come from thought while nonrational desires spring from other levels of awareness—appetites and feelings.

Rational desires are based on a level of cognitive ability available only to relatively mature human beings—the ability to reflect and to deliberate about what will be good for them. Rational desires aim at what human beings, after reflection and deliberation, have reason to believe is good for them. Nonrational desires, on the other hand, do not involve reasons for believing something is good. They simply aim, without reflection and deliberation, at whatever is pleasant or at whatever *appears* good. Animals, the Greeks thought, have nonrational desires. They have impulses and instincts to eat and to drink, to survive and to thrive, to fight and to flee, and to reproduce and to nurture their young. But animals are not capable of reflection and deliberation so they have no *reasons* to believe that what they pursue will be good for them. Their activities are driven by their impulses and instincts alone, and are thus the result of nonrational desires.

There was general agreement among the philosophers that human beings, and only human beings, have truly rational desires because only humans have a truly rational soul. There was also general agreement that animals have nonrational desires. The disagreement arose over whether human beings also have nonrational desires.

Humans frequently behave in ways similar to animals. Humans seek food when they are hungry and drink when they are thirsty, for example, so the question naturally arises: are these desires nonrational desires such as we find in animals, or are they rational desires, given that we find them in rational beings? In others words, do humans desire only what they have *reason* to believe is good (rational desires) or do they also desire some things simply because they are pleasurable or because they *appear* good (nonrational desires)? On this question the early virtue theorists differ. Some say that human beings have only rational desires; others say that we have nonrational desires as well.

Do People Have Nonrational Desires?

Socrates' View

Socrates holds that human beings have only rational desires. The desire for water when we are thirsty, therefore, is not a nonrational animal desire similar to what animals experience; rather, it is a uniquely human and rational desire. We do not desire water as animals do—simply because it is perceived as pleasant and good. Our desire for water is always accompanied by *reasons* for believing it is good for us. The human desire for water, according to Socrates, is a desire for water plus an evaluation—the reasonable belief that the water is actually good for us. If a human being believes that the water is not good (perhaps it is contaminated) then that person will, according to Socrates, no longer desire the water no matter how thirsty he or she is and how good it looks.

For Socrates, then, all our desires, even those we share with animals, are ultimately rational desires because reasoning is embedded in them. This helps explain Socrates' well-known view that virtue is knowledge and vice is ignorance; that is, a cognitive mistake. For Socrates, every human action is motivated by what the agent *thinks* is good for him or her, and thinking is something only humans can do. Unethical or immoral behavior—vice—never arises from nonrational desires overwhelming reason and knowledge. Rather, immoral behavior is always a cognitive mistake. It is rooted not in powerful nonrational drives but in ignorance. The person was doing what he or she thought was good; however, what one thought was good really was not. Nonrational desires are not the problem; the problem is ignorance. According to Socrates, human beings do not have nonrational desires.

Plato's View

Plato's view of desire is more complex. Unlike Socrates, he acknowledges that some behaviors of mature human beings spring from nonrational desires. Both Socrates and Plato think of the soul as the wellspring of human activity; however, unlike Socrates, Plato thinks of it as having "parts," some of which are not completely rational. In Book IV of the *Republic*, Plato outlines his well-known theory of the three parts of the human soul: the appetitive, the spirited, and the rational. Each part has its own desires. The appetitive (*epithumetikon*) part consists of urges and drives for pleasure; it desires whatever gives pleasure and it craves objects such as food, water, sex, power, and wealth. The spirited (*thumoeides*) part originates in the emotions; it desires whatever *appears* good in particular situations. When I have been hurt or victimized it may appear good to charge forward in anger, when faced with a dangerous situation it may appear good to recoil in fear, when a loved one dies it may appear good to wallow in unending grief, and so forth. The third part, the rational (*logistikon*) part, desires whatever is *truly* good. It desires not merely what is pleasurable or what appears good in a situation but what will be truly good for my life as a whole. The rational part relies on reasoning to decide in each situation whether activities that give pleasure—drinking water, for example—or activities that appear good—anger, fear, and grief, for example—will actually be good for my life considered as whole.

Both Socrates and Plato, then, think desires are at the source of ethical decision making. But they differ on a number of key points. Socrates thinks that all our desires are rational (if sometimes mistaken); Plato, on the other hand, acknowledges that we have some nonrational desires—those of the appetitive and spirited parts of the soul. For Socrates, when things go wrong it is due to ignorance. For Plato, when things go wrong it may be due to ignorance but it also may be due to nonrational desires overwhelming what we know to be truly good for us. For Socrates, ethics is totally rational; all we need to make good moral decisions is accurate knowledge. For Plato, ethics is more than rational; we need knowledge, but we also need to shape and form our nonrational desires by training, education, and the development of good habits, dispositions, and attitudes—what we today call moral character—because knowledge by itself is not enough to guide our strongest nonrational desires.

Plato's division of human psychology—the soul—into rational and irrational parts will have far-reaching consequences in the history of virtue ethics. It sets the stage for two kinds of virtues, what Aristotle will call intellectual virtue and character virtue. As we will see, in most modern accounts of virtue ethics the focus is almost exclusively on character virtues such as temperance, courage, justice, and love—virtues associated with such nonrational aspects of living as our appetites, our feelings, and our relationships with others. The ancients, however, do not give primacy to the character virtues that are relevant to the nonrational parts of the soul. They make intellectual virtue the fundamental and controlling virtue in ethics.

Aristotle's View

Aristotle follows the influential threefold division of the soul in Plato's *Republic*. He distinguishes three types of human desire, which he calls *orexis*, of which two are nonrational and one is rational. Appetite (*epithumia*) embraces nonrational physical desires for pleasurable activities such as eating, drinking, and sex. Emotion (*thumos*) embraces nonrational psychological desires such as anger, pride, shame, fear, caring, generosity, pity, and so forth. Aristotle calls these two types of nonrational desires *feelings*—we *feel* hungry, thirsty, and amorous, and we *feel* angry, shameful, generous, and so forth.

The third type of desire, rational desire, is not a feeling for what appears pleasant (the appetitive desires) or a feeling for what appears good at the time (the emotional desires). Rational desire is the *will* to achieve what we have reason to believe is truly good for us. Aristotle's word for rational desire is *boulesis* and a good translation of *boulesis* is "willing." Rational desire or willing is uniquely human because it involves reasoning and deliberation, and because it seeks what is truly good for the agent and not merely what is pleasant or what is apparently good.

For Aristotle, humans are fundamentally beings of desire (*orexis*). Our desires, both the nonrational feelings and the rational willings, generate our behavior. Aristotle thus agrees with Plato that ethics embraces both nonrational and rational desires, and that rational desire is more important because it seeks by intelligence and deliberation what is truly good, and not merely what is pleasant or apparently good, for the moral agent.

Stoic View

The Stoics disagree with Plato's and Aristotle's claim that the soul has nonrational parts. The Stoic soul is completely rational; it has no nonrational parts. What Plato and Aristotle called the appetites (hunger, thirst, and sexual craving) the Stoics attribute not to any part of the human soul but to the body. What Plato and Aristotle call emotion (anger, fear, grief, and so forth) and attribute to a nonrational part of the soul the Stoics simply attribute to the soul, which is totally rational.

They can attribute emotions to the rational soul because they view emotions as judgments about something or beliefs about something, and judgments and beliefs are rational activities. Anger is the belief that I should strike back, fear is the belief that harm will come, grief is the belief that I have lost something important, pity is the belief something terrible has happened, and so forth. The Stoics also believed that these emotions are *false* judgments and beliefs, and therefore that they should be rejected. For them, there is no question of cultivating and shaping the emotions according to reason, as there was for Plato and Aristotle. They believe that the emotions, false judgments and beliefs that they are, need to be rejected. Extirpating or rooting out the emotions (the passions) is a notoriously famous doctrine of the Stoics.

Despite this divergence from Plato and Aristotle on the psychology of the soul, the Stoics still root ethics in desire. The Stoics claim that our behavior originates in impulses that they called the *hormai*. We are born with basic impulses just as are animals, and many of our natural impulses are similar to those of animals. For example, both animals and humans have an impulse for self-preservation that gives rise to activities appropriate for taking in nourishment. As we mature another impulse shared with animals emerges: the impulse to reproduce and raise offspring, and this gives rise to appropriate sexual and parental activities. Because these impulses emerge in the body, we share them with animals.

Other impulses are uniquely human because they emerge in the rational soul. Only human beings, for example, have the impulse to develop oral and written languages. And, above all, human beings have rational impulses to develop knowledge about what is truly appropriate for human living. Rational impulses move us toward learning what behaviors are fitting and appropriate for rational beings.

The Stoic notion of "what is fitting or appropriate" (*oikeiosos*) for our rational natures is a key concept in their ethical theory. The word *oikeiosos* is often translated in the ethical literature as "appropriation." It connotes that something belongs to us by nature and is thus appropriate for us to pursue. Stoics call the behaviors that are naturally appropriate to us as rational beings the *kathekonta*.

Some modern references to Stoic ethics consider the "appropriate" behaviors (the *kathekonta*, the things that belong to us by nature) as synonymous with ethical behaviors. This is a misunderstanding that can be traced back to Cicero's commentaries on early Greek Stoicism. Cicero translated the Greek word *kathekonton* as *officium*, and the Latin word *officium* is then translated into English as "duty." The notion of duty is central in modern ethics, especially since Kant, so there is a tendency to interpret Cicero's *officia* as referring to our moral duties. Thus, the English translation of Cicero's *De Officiis* is often rendered (incorrectly) as the treatise on "Moral Duties." In fact, however, the *kathekonta* (what Cicero calls "duties") are a premoral notion in the ancient Stoic virtue ethics. The *kathekonta* or *officia* are not duties as we understand duty in English; the *kathekonta* are simply the things that are appropriate and fitting to our nature as human beings.

Moreover, the Stoics believe that not all "appropriate" behaviors (the *kathekonta*) are actually good for human beings. It is appropriate for us to engage in sex and reproduce, but not all sex and reproduction is good for us. It is appropriate for us to speak and write a language, but not all speaking and writing is good—words can be used to deceive, to belittle, to condemn, and so forth. Hence the Stoics identify a subset of "appropriate" human behaviors that they called "right actions" (the *katorthomata*). These "right actions" are those "appropriate actions" that are truly good for human beings and hence those that will be desired by all wise people. Stoic ethics centers on the *katorthomata*, the appropriate actions that are truly good for the person. Stoic ethics is about the *katorthomata* and not about the *kathekonta* or "duties."

Summary

Virtue ethics is about our behavior, about what we do. The energizing source of what we (and animals) do is desire or impulse. Some desires or impulses we share with animals—the desires for pleasure and for nurturing offspring, for example. Other desires are uniquely human—the desires or impulse to understand ourselves as well as the universe and to know what is truly good for our lives, for example.

Our natural desires and impulses are the starting points of virtue ethics. Socrates and the Stoics think that we have only rational desires and that the task of ethics is to ascertain that these desires are not hampered by ignorance and false beliefs. Plato and Aristotle, on the other hand, think that we have both nonrational and rational desires, and that the task of ethics is to shape and manage the nonrational desires as well as to eradicate ignorance and false beliefs.

Virtue ethics thus arises from the natural inclinations embedded in human nature. It is rooted in our natural desires for what is pleasurable and good, and hence differs from other major ethical theories in important ways. Virtue ethics is about desire and not duty, about what we want to do and not what we ought to do, about personal happiness and not the greatest happiness of all.

Two Objections

Many philosophers believe that locating the origin of ethics in our natural biological and psychological inclinations is a mistake. They argue that ethics is about obligation or what we ought to do, and that we can never get to this "ought" if we begin with the biological or psychological facts of nature. Any attempt to do so is what they sometimes call a "naturalistic" fallacy, the fallacy of attempting to derive moral obligations or values—what we ought to do—from facts we observe in human nature and culture. What we need, they argue, is some kind of starting point that transcends empirical human nature, perhaps divine law, or universal human rights, or what Kant called pure or transcendental reason—the impartial reason disengaged from our embodiment in a particular world of natural desires. But their objections about a naturalistic fallacy miss the point when they are leveled at ancient virtue ethics that makes no effort to go from "is" to "ought" because there is no "ought." Virtue ethics is not about obligation and what we ought to do, but about the good that is what we naturally desire. The Greeks are not guilty of the naturalistic fallacy of going from fact to value, from is to ought; they do not even attempt the jump. Values are embedded in what is, that is, in our biological and psychological striving to live a good life and to experience happiness and fulfillment in our lives.

Other philosophers object to what is called the teleological concept of human nature that emerges when ethics is based on an end that we desire. They understand this teleology to mean that human nature is directed to a goal or that it exists for a purpose. And this bothers them because it suggests various metaphysical positions that they consider unacceptable: that a deity designs and directs the universe, for example, or that some kind of master plan governs the appearance of species on earth, or that nature includes predetermined specific goals for natural beings, including human beings.

Yet teleology in ethics does not necessarily imply these positions. For Aristotle and the Stoics, for example, teleology simply means that an object functions well or poorly depending on whether or not it is achieving its appropriate *telos* or end. They think that the appropriate end for all beings is functioning well. Aristotle and the Stoics think of both artificial and natural beings, including human beings, as having appropriate functions. Artifacts, whether a simple object such as a hammer or a complex machine, obviously were designed to function in certain ways to accomplish certain tasks. When they function well and achieve their design goal, they are *good* hammers and *good* machines. But organic beings also function, and their natural functioning can be evaluated as well. Just as a machine functions well when it operates in accord with its designed end, an organic being functions well when it behaves in accord with its natural end. My arm functions well when it does what I expect a human arm to do. If it is broken, it does not function so well, or perhaps not at all. The same is true of my heart, my lungs, my kidneys, my liver, indeed, of my whole being in all its dimensions. Humans are thus achieving their end—happiness—

whenever the physical, psychological, interpersonal, social, and political aspects of their lives are functioning well and harmoniously. Teleology, in what is known as Aristotle's famous "function argument," simply means that organisms are a work (*ergon*) in progress—a process. Living beings are, in a sense, incomplete. Embedded in their nature are numerous unrealized capabilities or capacities, and they function well when they actualize those innate natural capabilities that make their lives go well. Most objections to teleology—functioning toward a goal—are directed toward a teleology that posits an extrinsic goal somehow directing the organism. Aristotle's teleology posits an intrinsic goal—the notion of having an end simply means that an organism has a natural tendency to function well, to "do well." Living well is our end, and the inclination to do well and live well is our natural teleology. Because human beings are rational beings, they function well only when they are actualizing their rational potential to manage their own lives intelligently. We achieve the goal of living good lives by guiding our lives with knowledge and reason. According to Aristotle, proper human functioning is the "actualization of the soul according to reason or involving reason" (NE 1098a7–8).

Greek teleology thus does not imply a designer-deity; it merely states that the human organism's natural function is to seek, with reason and intelligence, ends or goals such as self-preservation, offspring, language, knowledge, community, wisdom, contemplation, and so forth. Teleology, so understood, is compatible with Charles Darwin's idea of natural selection, which explains that species originate and survive thanks to organisms functioning well enough to reproduce offspring with features enabling them to fit well—that is, to do well and reproduce—in their environment. And it is also compatible with modern molecular biology, which seeks to understand how the biological processes from the level of the gene through the proteins they produce direct the development and functioning of each organism.

Both evolutionary and molecular biology suggest that life naturally develops and functions so as to achieve ends. The process of natural selection suggested by Darwin, despite the generation of numerous individuals and species that fail to fit the environment, can be seen as a process tending toward an end—the survival of species. And the genes embedded in the cells of living beings, despite some deleterious mutations, can also be seen as tending toward an end—the well-being of the organism. Aristotle's teleology is similar; it simply suggests that living beings have a tendency to survive and to flourish, and that humans do this best when they function as rational beings and live intelligently.

Desires, Impulses, and Good Things

We have seen that the roots of virtue ethics lie in our natural desires and impulses. In common with other sentient animals, human beings are beings of desire. We want things—we want food, companionship, money, comfort, pleasure, supportive social and political environments, recognition, fair play, love, health care, education, and so forth. We desire these things because they are pleasurable or perceived as good. Aristotle begins his *Nicomachean Ethics* with this famous sentence:

> Everything we make and every inquiry, and likewise every action and decision, seem to aim at some good; hence it has been well said that all these (behaviors) aim at the good. (NE 1094a1–3)

If we are thirsty we seek fluid, if we are in pain we seek relief, if we feel unappreciated we seek recognition, if we are wronged by others we seek compensation, and so forth. Not every goal we desire, however, is truly good for us. Sometimes what we desire looks good but in reality is not good for us. To the shipwrecked sailor dying of thirst the ocean water may look good to drink, but it is not.

The difference between what is apparently good and what is actually good is easy to see in reference to our appetites—the food or sex we crave may not be good for us although it appears good—but the distinction may not be so clear when it applies to the emotional and rational domains of our lives. Becoming angry after being wronged is a natural response but it may not be a good move in some situations. Even the desire to engage extensively in the pursuit of knowledge or wisdom—to become a scientist or a philosopher—may appear good to a person but not really be good for him.

Quite simply, often what we think will be good for us may not be good for us. Hence a major task in life is figuring out which of our desired objectives are truly, and not just apparently, good. Whenever we begin figuring out what is truly good for ourselves we are beginning our engagement with virtue ethics.

The distinction between what is apparently good for us and what is actually good for us enables us to avoid confusing the good as the Greeks understood it with the good as some contemporary thinkers understand it. Today, some have the tendency to identify the good with whatever we happen to desire or to think is in our interest. The good is understood in terms of choice—each person has the right to choose, and whatever she chooses is good for her. Whatever appears good to a person is thus whatever he or she thinks is good for them.

Virtue ethics rejects this position. The most we can say about our initial desires and impulses is that they aim at what *appears* good. Before we can say that the objects of these desires are truly good we need to examine them and think critically about them; we need to see whether we have reasons for believing that they are truly good for us.

The ancient language of "the good" and "good things" may seem a little awkward today. If so, you can think of words such as "value" and "valuable" whenever you see the words "good" and "good things" in the literature of virtue ethics. Desiring "the good" is desiring the valuable, desiring "good things" is desiring whatever is valuable. Virtue ethics is about values, about the value that is life and about what is valuable for living life well. Of course, not everything that appears valuable to us is actually valuable, and figuring out what is truly valuable before we choose is the business of ethics. A core assumption of virtue ethics, as we will see, is that intelligent choices—choices mediated by practical wisdom and prudence—will tend to be better choices than those made without intelligence and deliberation.

Self-Interest and the Good

The good each person desires in virtue ethics is primarily his own good. It is not the good in general, nor the good for all mankind, nor the good for the greatest number, nor the good for another human being, although these goods are often integral to the person's good. Seeking one's own personal good is clearly an exercise in self-interest and self-concern. Seeking the "good" is seeking the "good for me." As we will see, however, the "me" in the "good for me" is actually a "we." The Greeks insisted that human life is by nature an interpersonal and political life. Thus "my" good is also an interpersonal and political good—the good of others and the good of the community. Although the good I desire is always my good, it will often be good for me to seek the good of others and the good of the community.

In the dialogue known as the *Euthydemus*, Socrates asks whether everyone wants "to do well" in life and then immediately admits that the question is a silly one because obviously everyone wants to do well in life (*Euthd.* 279E3–6). Then he asks whether doing well is achieving what is good for the person and immediately acknowledges that this question is even more silly than the first because it is also obvious that a person does well by achieving what is good for himself (*Euthd.* 280A1–3). This interest that each person has to achieve what is good for herself is the basis of Socrates' approach to ethics. For him it is obvious that the good we seek is our personal good. What is not so obvious, of course, is figuring out how to achieve our good. In the *Euthydemus* Socrates goes on to make the famous claim that the only thing a person really needs to achieve his personal good is knowledge of what is truly good for humans.

The issue of self-interest also emerges sharply in Aristotle. For Aristotle the good of any being, including human beings, lies in actualizing its natural capacities. Human life is a goal-directed activity where the goal is actualizing our potential for self-realization. Achieving a good life requires fulfilling capacities inherent in human nature in a specifically human way; that is, by choosing intelligently what is truly good for ourselves. Desiring and achieving what is good for ourselves, the mark of a good man, is obviously desiring and accomplishing what is in our self-interest.

> [The good person] desires for himself goods and whatever show themselves as goods (*ta phainomena*), and actually brings these about (since working for the good is the mark of a good man), and he does this for his sake (for he does it thanks to thinking it over, the very thing which seems to mark each good

person.) And he desires life and self-preservation, and desires this most of all for that part of himself whereby he is in possession of his senses. For living is a good for the good person, and each person desires goods for himself. (NE 1166a14–20)

It is important to understand this notion of self-interest correctly. It does not mean, as it does in some modern ethics, that it is good for a person to satisfy whatever interests or preferences she happens to have. The Greeks were very clear that something does not become good for us simply because we desire it; rather, we desire it because we think it truly good. Our self-interest, rightly understood, is achieving what is truly good, and not simply getting what we happen to want. Self-interest for the Greeks was not understood as some understand it today, that is, as the satisfaction of our preferences and desires, whatever they happen to be.

The language of self-interest—the desire to achieve the good things that will make one's life good—obviously introduces some tension between virtue ethics and the various forms of obligation ethics. Both traditional religious ethics as well as modern theories of deontology and utilitarianism center ethics on the interests of others. Altruism, forgetting ourselves for the sake of others, has long been an ideal in Christian ethics. Impartiality, remembering ourselves but not counting ourselves more than other selves, is a characteristic assumption in both Kantian and utilitarian ethics. What, then, can be said about the slant toward self-interest embedded in virtue ethics? Virtue ethics seems to encourage egoism instead of altruism and partiality toward oneself instead of impartiality. Does virtue ethics encourage egoism and self-preference, attitudes and actions that are deplored by most moral theology and moral philosophy? Is not one of the problems with virtue ethics that it moves too far toward personal good, and that it is self-centered, when ethics should be more about universal principles and how we treat others?

Virtue ethics is clearly agent relative. Virtue ethics is rooted in the instincts and desires of each person to make her life a good life. And the good it advocates is the personal good of the moral agent. The goal for each person is to make the choices that will make her life go well. But it is anachronistic to conclude that virtue ethics is partial to oneself or egoistic in any objectionable sense. In virtue ethics, the tilt toward self-interest is not identified with immoral self-concern but with a psychological reality. My desires are first of all desires that my life goes well. As we shall see, this is a morally admirable attitude when it is correctly understood.

Moreover, the distinctions between egoism and altruism, and between partiality to self and impartiality, with the implication that we must make a choice between one or the other, is a way of thinking that is markedly absent in ancient ethical texts, where no lengthy discussions of dichotomies such as egoism-altruism, partiality-impartiality, are to be found. Hence, it is anachronistic to think in terms of dichotomies such as egoism-altruism or partiality-impartiality when talking of ancient virtue ethics.

The originators of virtue ethics do not conceive of an individual self as somehow distinct from other selves and from its social and political environments. Rather, each individual is conceived as a complex self, a self that is an individual constituted by its choices and also as a social being constituted by its interpersonal and political relationships. "My life" is not conceived in virtue ethics as a single life complete in itself but as an interpersonal and political life. To focus above all on "my life" is to focus on "my-life-with-others-in-political-communities." The original virtue ethicists see no sharp distinction between my self-interest and the interests of others who are also pursuing truly good lives, and they think that it is often in my self-interest to pursue the interests of others.

Thus, a choice does not have to be made between pursuing my self-interest and the interests of others; it is in my self-interest to pursue the interests of others, not because they are a means to my interests but because my interest is to pursue their interests. Being interested in and concerned for others for their sake is, somewhat paradoxically, in my self-interest. Treating other people well need not mean treating them as a means to further my interest; it may mean, and in virtue ethics it does mean, that it is in my self-interest to treat them well for their own sake.

The Overriding Good

The Greeks think that human beings, indeed all sentient beings, naturally desire what they perceive as good or valuable for themselves. A significant question now arises: Are the individual goods that we seek in our various projects and activities the only goods we seek or is there also an overriding good in life? Are there only particular and discrete goods in our lives or is there a universal and general good? Do we seek only goods embedded in various projects and activities or is there a highest good that supersedes the good of specific projects and behaviors? In addition to the many particular goods we seek in life is there, to use the traditional language of philosophers, an *akrotaton agathon*, a *summum bonum* (a highest good, a greatest good, the best good, *the* good, and so forth) and, if there is, what is it and how do we achieve it?

The question haunted the Greeks and still haunts moral philosophy today. John Stuart Mill notes on the first page of his seminal book *Utilitarianism*, published in 1863: "From the dawn of philosophy, the question concerning the *summum bonum*, or, what is the same thing, concerning the foundation of morality, has been accounted the main problem in speculative thought." In the century before him, Kant, at the end of the *Critique of Pure Reason* (A 803, B 831), insisted that the *summum bonum* determines the ultimate aim of pure reason and provides what I can hope to achieve if I do what I ought to do. Hence, both Mill and Kant, founding fathers of contemporary utilitarian and deontological ethics, respectively, acknowledge the central role of a *summum bonum* or a highest and overriding good.

Before elaborating on the overall good in virtue ethics, we need to note several things. First, the notion of the "highest good" is a very complex and somewhat ambiguous notion in Greek philosophy. The surviving texts are not as clear as we would like; furthermore, some important texts, such as Plato's *On the Good,* have been lost. Extensive debates over the meaning of "the good" in Greek philosophy have existed since the ancient times and they continue to this day. These scholarly debates are important but beyond the scope of this introductory text.

Second, the word "good" is notoriously ambiguous in modern English. Sometimes, it actually means something bad. A radiologist might speak of a "good-sized tumor" when neither the tumor nor its size is really good at all for the patient. A police officer might speak of a driver "going at a good clip" when the speed is not good legally, and its capture on radar will not be good for the driver. A homeowner might spot water under the hot water tank and then discover "a real good leak" that is not good at all. A city firefighter might talk of some "good fires" that have been fought recently, yet these fires are not really good events.

Third, the notion of an overriding good presupposes that we view our lives not simply as a series of discrete experiences but as a whole. Each life is a single story and the objective is to make the whole story a good story. All the major Greek philosophers think that we should view life as a whole and thus seek an overriding good for life with but one exception—a fringe group known as the Cyrenaics. They reject the idea of achieving any overall or long-term goal for life as a whole. The only goods we seek are particular goods—the pleasures of the moment. They find no reason to seek an overriding good for life. The Cyrenaics had little influence on ancient ethics. Their unabashed hedonism, which ignored concern for one's life as a whole or for other people, never impressed many thinking people as a viable ethics.

Fourth, the notion of the "highest good" or "*the* good" cuts across two major domains in philosophy: practical philosophy and theoretical philosophy. Ethics is a practical philosophy that tries to guide human action; theoretical philosophy (later called metaphysics) tries to explain the nature of things or beings. In ethics, the "highest good" refers to what reasonable human beings desire most for their lives; in theoretical philosophy, the "highest good" refers to notions such as the best being (Aristotle's divine unmoved mover) or even to something beyond all beings (Plato's Idea or Form of "the Good").

The relation between the theoretical concepts of the highest good and the practical concepts—the *summum bonum* of ethics—is difficult to understand. In texts such as the *Republic*, Plato feels that we have to know of the highest good, the Good itself, if we are going to understand and define the practical good in ethics.

Aristotle, however, considers Plato's Idea of "the Good" irrelevant for ethics. Yet, at the end of *Eudemian Ethics*, Aristotle speaks of God, which he described in metaphysical terms as the Unmoved Mover in his theoretical books, *Physics* and *Metaphysics*—as if theoretical knowledge of God were relevant to ethics:

Whatever choice and possession of natural goods—whether bodily goods, or wealth, or friends, or other goods—will best promote the contemplation of God is the best good, and this is the finest standard; and whatever through deficiency or excess hinders us from serving and contemplating God, that is bad. (EE 1249b17–21)

Despite Aristotle's insistence that ethics is about activity rather than theory, his statement is not surprising once we remember that the highest activity in a human being is thinking, and that the highest form of thinking is theoretical or contemplative thinking, and that the highest object we can think about theoretically or contemplatively is the First Unmoved Mover or God. Thus, the best of human activities is engaging in theoretical knowledge and contemplation of God. Furthermore, this recognition will have a bearing on our moral choices.

Finally, the Stoics link ethics with the theoretical study of nature (which they called physics and understood to be the study of the world unfolding according to a benevolent logical plan) and insist that ethical action is action "according to nature." Plutarch quotes Chrysippus as saying: "there is no other or more appropriate way of approaching the study of good and bad things or the virtues or happiness but from universal nature and from the administration of the world" (Long and Sedley, *The Hellenistic Philosophers*, 2:364).

Just what role the notions of the good in metaphysics or theology should play in ethics is a tangled web in ancient philosophy. We need to leave the controversies aside, however, and focus on the overriding good or the greatest good that is directly relevant to ethics.

Plato and the Overriding Good

In Plato's early dialogues, the question of the overriding good or *summum bonum* emerges when we see Socrates searching for definitions of some popular virtues—piety in the *Euthyphro*, temperance in the *Charmides*, and courage in the *Laches*. Definitions of the virtues are important because they move beyond particular instances to a universal essence that is exemplified in all the particular instances. One of the most intriguing things about Plato's early dialogues, however, is that Socrates never really gets good definitions expressing the essential characteristics of virtues such as piety, temperance, and courage. He sees the need for definitions that move beyond individual acts of piety for example, to a universal property that defines the essence of piety itself, but he never succeeds in formulating them.

Plato thinks that Socrates' failure to develop definitions can be traced to his failure to see that no real universal definition of anything in this sensible world is possible because all things in this sensible world are particular things and subject to change. The solution, Plato thinks, is to invoke a nonsensible world—the world of Platonic Forms or Ideas where the realities are universal Forms that do not change. In Book IV of the *Republic* we find Socrates (now really Plato) giving some definitions of the four major virtues (wisdom, justice, temperance, and courage) by appealing to knowledge of the corresponding nonsensible transcendent Forms of these virtues. These Platonic Forms or Ideas are universal and unchanging realities existing in a realm transcending the sensible realm of space, time, and matter. They are perceived or, more accurately, remembered by the mind. Knowledge of the Ideas or Forms is the kind of knowledge that allows us to give definitions. Definitions describe the essential permanent features of all particulars covered by the definitions. Definitions provide universal and unchanging descriptions. Knowledge of the Ideas or Forms provides this kind of knowledge and permits Socrates to give the definitions of individual virtues such as justice and courage in the *Republic*.

Plato does not stop with universal definitions of the individual virtues; that is, with the knowledge of what wisdom, justice, courage, and temperance really are, which is something our soul remembers from its life before it entered the body. In Book VI of the *Republic*, he has Socrates tell us that these definitions derived from the Ideas presuppose a knowledge of something more fundamental than even the Ideas of the individual virtues. They presuppose knowledge of a superior Idea—the Idea of the Good itself. This is so because the virtues as well as other beneficial things are all good, and hence the definitions of the virtues and beneficial things presuppose some knowledge of a more universal Idea—the Idea of the Good.

Socrates' companions, Glaucon and Adeimantus, press him to give a definition of this superior Idea—the Idea of the Good—just as he had given definitions of the virtues in Book IV. He declines, saying that he is unable to give such explanations (*Rep.* 506D). The Idea of the Good is not like the other Ideas/Forms, in fact, it is "beyond being" (*Rep.* 509B) and hence cannot be defined. Nonetheless, he says, we can gain some knowledge of it by analogy. The Good, says Plato, is like the light of the sun. As light enables us to see other objects but is not itself a visible object, the Good enables us to define the virtues and other good things but is not itself definable.

In the *Republic,* Plato makes the transcendent Idea of "the Good" the highest good, what later philosophy called the *summum bonum.* This good transcends both the particular virtuous actions that we observe in the world and the transcendent Ideas or Forms of the virtues that are not observed but known by the mind. There is thus a double step toward the universal in Plato's ethics. First, the individual instances of a virtue, courage, for example, point to the universal Idea "courage" and the knowledge of this Idea enables us to define courage. Second, the universal Ideas of the virtues (courage, justice, and so forth) point to the greater universal Idea of "the Good" that is presupposed in all the Ideas of the virtues.

To some, Plato's highest good—the transcendent Idea of the Good itself—seems irrelevant to ethics. Indeed, Aristotle criticizes it for just this reason, claiming (NE 1096b31–35) that Plato's Idea of the Good is not an object of our desires and hence could not be the overriding good of ethics. What we desire, he says, are good things (*ta agatha*) that actually help us live well (*eu zen*) and not abstractions such as the universal Idea of the Good.

Yet ethics is never far from Plato's mind in the *Republic.* The discussion of the Idea of the Good in Book VI was generated by the account of the major virtues in Book IV, and virtues are obviously connected with the practical side of life. Moreover, the Idea of the Good in Book VI is immediately linked with a discussion of the good that everyone wants most in their lives (*Rep.* 505E). This link of "the Good" with the personal good of each person makes "the Good" relevant to ethics. It seems that Plato thinks that the Idea of the Good, while beyond all being and hence not definable, is nonetheless somehow relevant to the practical concerns of our lives.

As the discussion about the nature of the practical good that everyone seeks in life unfolds in Book VI, Socrates immediately rejects two common proposals: the overriding good we are all seeking cannot be pleasure and it also cannot be, despite what Socrates had suggested in the earlier dialogues, simply knowledge. Just what does Plato think is the overriding good in this life? No clear conception emerges in the *Republic*.

Plato's conception of the overriding practical good finally emerges more clearly in a later dialogue titled the *Philebus*. The question of the highest good in this dialogue is clearly a question about the highest good in human life as it is lived and not about the Idea of the Good grasped by recollection. Perhaps Plato has become aware of Aristotle's critique of the Idea of the Good in the *Republic* by this time. In the *Philebus,* the overriding good governing how we should live does not exist in the transcendent realm of Ideas but in everything that is good for human life. The *Philebus* represents what is arguably Plato's most important surviving treatment of the greatest good relevant to ethics.

The dialogue begins with a dispute between Socrates and Philebus about what is the most important good in a human life. Philebus says that it is pleasure and Socrates says that it is prudence (*phronesis*). Suddenly, after arguing against pleasure and defending prudence, Socrates reverses his position and states that the overriding good in life is neither pleasure nor prudence but something else altogether that is superior to both (*Phil.* 20B). He then leads another discussant, Protarchus, to agree on what the essential characteristics of this overriding good would have to be. From this conversation we learn that the greatest good in life will have to be in some sense "complete" and "adequate" and what everyone wants (*Phil.* 20D). Scholars disagree somewhat on just what "complete" (*teleon*) and "adequate" (*ikanon*) mean here, but the basic idea seems to be this: the highest and overriding practical good will be *complete* in the sense that it will embrace all the important goods in life and *adequate* in the sense that it will satisfy all our impulses and desires.

Accepting the characteristic of completeness shows that neither pleasure nor prudence is enough because neither by itself will make a human life complete. Socrates argues that the highest good must therefore include both pleasure and prudence. In other words, the highest good is mixed—a combination of feeling and knowledge (*Phil.* 21A). And the second highest good, according to Socrates, is prudence itself (*phronesis*) because prudence is the knowledge that regulates the mixture of feelings and knowledge. Despite his earlier tendency in the *Republic* to stress the nonsensible character of the highest good, Plato is now making it clear that the overriding good in human life lies in a mixed reality, a combination of prudence and pleasure, with the former regulating the latter.

This is a rather startling development in Plato's thought. His theoretical philosophy had displaced ultimate reality to a metaphysical realm that was beyond our sensible world and in which individual beings exist as copies of the transcendent Ideas or Forms. In the *Republic*, a middle dialogue, discussion about the ultimate good led to the universal Idea of the Good in the metaphysical realm that was beyond all definition. But in the *Philebus,* the ultimate good in ethics is brought back to the world of space and time. The overriding good that we desire in our lives is no longer the Idea of the Good but a life actually lived well, and a life lived well is a life of pleasure guided by prudence. The metaphysical Idea of the Good is not rejected; it is simply ignored in the discussion about the highest good in human life.

Aristotle and the Overriding Good

Aristotle's approach to the question of the overriding good bears some striking similarities to Plato's account in the *Philebus*. He agrees, for example, that the overriding good will have to be "complete" or "final" (*teleion,* a variant spelling of *teleon*) and it will have to be "self-sufficient" (*autarkes*).

Aristotle explains what he means by "complete" or "final" by noting that we can seek goals in three different ways. We might seek a goal not for its own sake but for the sake of another goal (getting a hammer to drive a nail, for example). We might also seek a goal for the sake of another goal and also for its own sake as well (buying a sports car that I will enjoy driving but will also use for business travel, for example). Finally, we might seek a goal simply for its own sake. This kind of goal is a final goal because it is sought only for its own sake. The overriding good will be the "absolutely final" goal that one can seek in life, the final and complete goal of living.

> We speak of what is sought for its own sake as more complete and final than what is sought for the sake of something else, and what is never chosen for the sake of something else is more complete and final than what is chosen both for its own sake and also for the sake of something else, and hence what is always chosen for its own sake and never for the sake of something else is "absolutely final" (*aplos teleion*). (NE 1097a30–33)

The overriding goal will also be "self-sufficient." What does Aristotle mean by this? Simply that it is all we need to make our lives good: "By self-sufficient (*autarkes*) we mean what all by itself makes life desirable and lacking nothing" (NE 1097b14–15). The highest good in ethics will embrace whatever is needed to make a life go well. For Aristotle the highest good includes pleasure and prudence as well as other goods such as health and financial resources. "There are three kinds of goods: external goods, goods of the soul, and goods of the body" (NE 1098b13–14). Aristotle's overriding good is similar to Plato's good in the *Philebus*—it is a practical good that is final, complete, and sufficient for making a human life go well.

All the major virtue theorists after Aristotle continue to make a notion of the highest good central to their ethics. Their descriptions of this overriding good are similar to those developed by Plato and Aristotle. Perhaps the best source for seeing the continuing concern with the overriding good after Aristotle is Cicero's book with the almost indecipherable title *Ends of Goods and Evils* (*De Finibus Bonorum et Malorum*), known simply as the *De Finibus*. Fortunately, the text makes the book's title clear. Cicero is explaining to a Roman readership in the first century B.C.E. the three prominent virtue theories he had studied in Athens and Rhodes: Epicureanism, Stoicism, and the views of Antiochus of Ascalon, a contemporary of Cicero. The plural "goods and evils" simply indicates that Cicero is presenting several theories of good and evil, and the word "ends" indicates that Cicero is explaining the ultimate or final good and evil in each system. In other words, a modern idiomatic rendering of Cicero's elusive title could be "Theories about the Greatest Good and the Worst Evil."

The subject of the book is: "What is the final and ultimate end to which all deliberations of living well and behaving rightly are to be referred?" (*De Finibus* I, iv). The Epicurean theory of the final end is presented and criticized in Books I and II, the Stoic version is presented and criticized in Books III and IV, and Antiochus' version is presented and criticized in Book V. We learn from Cicero that all three theories agree that there is a *summum bonum*, the highest good, and its characteristics are "final" and "ultimate" (*extremum* and *ultimum*; *De Finibus* I, iv; III, vii; V, vi). The final and ultimate *summum bonum* is something to which everything should be referred yet it refers to nothing (*De Finibus* I, ix). It is praiseworthy and desirable for its own sake, it is the good to which all else is referred (*De Finibus* III, vi). In the *De Finibus,* Cicero leaves no doubt about the central role of the overriding good (the final and ultimate end) in every ethical theory he studied.

There is thus widespread agreement in ancient virtue ethics not only that every action and decision are aiming at some good but also that all our actions and decisions are aiming at some kind of overriding good. This is what Aristotle calls the "highest good" (the *agathon akrotaton* [NE 1095a17]), and what becomes known in succeeding centuries of moral philosophy (as the writings of such seminal figures as Kant and Mill attest) as the *summum bonum*. The good sought in ethics is, in the last analysis, not any particular good but an overriding good. What is ultimately good is not any particular external good such as wealth, nor any good of the body such as sensual pleasure, nor any good of the soul such as knowledge. The overriding good, the *summum bonum*, is whatever makes the whole of human life good. Virtue ethics focuses primarily on life as a whole and only then on particular actions and behaviors.

Summary of the Starting Point (the *Arche*) of Greek Virtue Ethics

It is time to summarize what we have learned about the origins of virtue ethics. The Greeks called the origin or starting point of anything its "principle" (*arche*). The principle of anything is its beginning; thus "arche-ology" is the study of beginnings. The English word "principle" comes from the Latin *principium,* which also means beginning.

We have to be careful of the word "principle" here. In modern ethics the notion of principle signifies some kind of moral rule, law, or guide derived from some moral theory or from past cases and then applied to a particular action so we can judge whether the action is right or wrong. In virtue ethics the principle is not something derived from theory or precedent but it is the source and beginning from which all else is derived. In virtue ethics, the word "principle" does not denote a derived guideline for particular actions; it denotes the starting point for thinking about life as a whole.

We can summarize the important features of this starting point—the first principle of virtue ethics—as follows. First, it is rooted in nature. The origin of virtue ethics lies in the instincts, desires, and impulses of human nature. We humans are beings of desire, and our desires initiate and sustain our behaviors. Seeking what is good for us is natural—the desire for the good is rooted in human nature. What gets ethics going is our natural instincts, desires, and impulses for something good that we need and do not have. Some of these instincts and desires are analogous to those of animals. Others, such as our desire to know and understand, are uniquely human.

Second, human beings desire not only particular goods—food when hungry, justice when wronged—but an overriding good, the most important good making our lives as a whole good. This overriding good is the *summum bonum*—the final, complete, satisfying, self-sufficient, and ultimately most desirable goal. Success or failure in life depends on how well we understand and achieve this overriding goal. Each human life is a narrative with a central character whose life unfolds in many chapters linked by the underlying question: will she manage her life so that it goes well?

Third, the overriding good sought by human beings is intensely and unabashedly personal. The good I seek is my good, the life I manage is my life. Virtue ethics is agent-centered—the starting point is not my concern for others but my concern for my life. However, as we shall see, my life will not go well unless I behave well toward others.

Fourth, recognizing that we are beings of desire reveals that we are, as are all living beings, incomplete. We have needs to satisfy and potentials to realize, and our instincts and desires propel us toward their fulfillment. The Greeks think of all living beings, including human beings, as beings who need to complete themselves. Living is the process of striving to realize our potential and fulfill our desire for a good life. This fulfillment is not something that comes after life is lived but is the successful living of life itself. The overriding good we seek is integral to life; it is what completes and satisfies our natural desire to live well as we actually live day by day.

We now need to explain what we have been calling the overriding good of human life. We need to know more about what it is and what constitutes it. Fortunately the originators of virtue ethics share a general agreement about what to call this overriding good. They call it *happiness*. Aristotle puts it well when he writes:

> What is the highest good sought in all our actions? As far as the name goes there is agreement among most people, for both the general public and educated people say it is happiness (*eudaimonia*), and they consider living well (*eu zen*) and doing well (*eu prattein*) the same as being happy. (NE 1095a17–21)

According to Aristotle only happiness can be called the greatest good. It is the only thing that we desire solely for its own sake and not for the sake of anything else. There are other things that we desire for their own sakes—things such as pleasure, intelligence (*nous*), and the moral virtues. But we desire these things also for the sake of something else—happiness. Pleasure, intelligence, and moral virtue are of little value to us if they do not bring happiness. Again, Aristotle puts it well:

> Happiness, more than anything, is absolutely final. For we always choose it for the sake of itself and never for the sake of

something else, while honor and pleasure and understanding and every virtue, although we certainly choose them for the sake of themselves (for we would choose each of them even if nothing more resulted), we also choose them for the sake of happiness, thinking that through these we will be happy. But no one chooses happiness for the sake of these or for the sake of anything else. (NE 1097a35–b7)

The overriding good of Greek ethics is happiness. The master goal of living—the best good we can seek for our lives—is living well and doing well, and this they call happiness. The next chapter will consider how the virtue theorists understand happiness, the greatest good we can hope to achieve in our lives. Cicero sums up the importance of the highest good in Greek ethics as follows:

When the highest good (*summum bonum*) is settled in philosophy everything is settled. . . . If the highest good is not known the guide for living our lives cannot be known; and the result of this error is that people are not able to know where they should take refuge. However, after the ends of things are known, and when what is the ultimate good and ultimate evil is understood, a way of life is discovered. (*De Finibus* V, vi)

CHAPTER 2

Happiness

The Greatest Good Is Happiness

The Greek philosophers insist that our desires aim ultimately at an overriding good, that this overriding good is the greatest good, that the greatest good is a good life, and that a good life is a life of happiness (*eudaimonia*). There is only one exception to this view: the Cyrenaics held that we do not desire any overriding good for our lives as a whole but only particular goods, which they identify with pleasure. All the other philosophers, however, hold that we do desire an overriding good for our lives as a whole and that the word describing this greatest good is happiness.

Because the Cyrenaics were a short-lived fringe group, we can say that all the important early Greek ethicists consider happiness the greatest good. They argue that happiness is the only good that we seek both for its own sake and never for the sake of anything else. There are other goods that we seek for their own sakes—the virtues, for example—but the philosophers claim that we seek these goods *also* for the sake of happiness. Happiness, however, is the one good we seek *only* for its own sake. Happiness is not a stepping stone to anything else; it is the ultimate final goal of human desire.

The moral philosophers did not invent the notion of happiness. Long before they appeared at the end of the fifth century B.C.E., people were thinking about and desiring *eudaimonia*, that is, a "good fate" (*eu-daimon*) in life. However, they were rather pessimistic about achieving it. They thought a good fate or a happy life was relatively rare. Few people got to live lives of happiness, and if one happened to have such a life they thought it was largely the result of luck.

What the philosophers do is build on the popular prephilosophical notion of happiness. Ultimately, they transform it by linking happiness to our deliberate choices. They claim that developing virtue in our lives by choosing wisely will eliminate or at least reduce the role of luck in achieving happiness. Happiness is up to us; achieving it depends on the decisions we make.

Socrates and the Stoics think that happiness is solely up to the individual—the truly virtuous person will be happy no matter how much bad luck and tragedy strike her or his life. Plato's position is more complicated. He first thought that he could make happiness immune to luck; however, he subsequently acknowledges that a full life needs not just contemplation but passion, and happiness is at risk once we acknowledge that passion is a crucial component of a happy and fulfilled life. In the *Republic,* for example, Plato argued that earthly happiness consists in the contemplation of the eternal Forms, which will render us immune to luck in life; however, in the later *Phaedrus,* Plato has Socrates admit that passion, with its risks, plays an indispensable role in human happiness. Clearly, Plato comes to see that happiness is subject to some factors beyond human control. Aristotle adopts this general position and does not hesitate to acknowledge that bad luck and tragedy can undermine the happiness of virtuous people. The most Plato and Aristotle can say, then, is that happiness is largely up to us but there are no guarantees that making good decisions will inevitably result in a happy life.

Making happiness or a good life depend, at least to some extent, on our deliberate choices revises the prephilosophical notion of happiness in several unexpected ways. To understand the philosophers' revisions, we need to look first at the general prephilosophical notion of happiness and also at the various definitions of happiness that had been proposed before the philosophers began their work. Only then can we see how both the popular notion and the early definitions were transformed as the philosophers develop the philosophical conception of happiness that lies at the root of virtue ethics.

The Prephilosophical Notion of Happiness

In ancient Greece the general notion of happiness among people was similar to what people have in mind today when, for example, they wish newly married people happiness or when, as parents, they hope their children will find happiness in life. The word happiness in these examples connotes a flourishing and fulfilling life, something quite close to what *eudaimonia* meant to the ancient Greek people. Analysis of this general prephilosophical notion of happiness reveals several important features that the philosophers will later develop. It will be useful to identify five of these features.

Happiness Is a Network

Happiness consists in many interconnected "good things" or "goods" (*agatha*) and presupposes the absence of "bad things." Happiness so understood is not one single thing but a collage of numerous different goods without too many bad things. Among the goods are health, wealth, pleasure, family, honors, and so forth. In the popular conception happiness is a collective noun designating a set of goods.

Happiness Endures over Time

Happiness is a life that runs its course well year after year. It is not a fleeting or transitory phenomenon but a long-term reality. A happy person fares well and flourishes as life unfolds. Things work out well for him or her in the long run.

Happiness Is Both Subjective and Objective

A person living a happy life not only *thinks* he or she is happy, but, in fact, his or her life *is* truly a happy life. It is important to stress the objective side of happiness because the word "happy" so often means little more than the experience of feeling happy in some contemporary conversations. Among the Greeks, happiness was more than feeling happy; it meant that the life of the person feeling happy was actually going well.

Happiness Is What One Desires Most in Life

There is nothing better, nothing more good, than happiness. When we have happiness our greatest human desire is satisfied. Beyond happiness there is nothing to seek. It makes no sense to ask why we want happiness or to live well because no one seeks happiness for the sake of anything else. Happiness, in the popular conception, is the one thing we desire only for its own sake.

Happiness Requires Freedom and Knowledge

A happy life is a life lived by a free person. People cannot achieve happiness unless they have some significant control over their lives. Long before the philosophers appeared, people recognized that freedom was essential for happiness. We can see this in one of Plato's dialogues that records a conversation between Socrates and a boy named Lysis who is still living at home and studying with a tutor. Lysis speaks for most Greeks when he says that no one can be happy unless he is free. Socrates then notes that this claim sets up an apparent contradiction: How can Lysis claim that his parents want him to achieve happiness, as they do, yet deprive him of his freedom by making him obey them (*Lysis* 207e–210c)? Lysis says that his parents will not give him the freedom to manage his own life because he is not old enough. Socrates dismisses this response and leads Lysis to the correct one: the real reason his parents do not give him his freedom is not because he is too young but because he does not yet possess the knowledge to choose wisely. Happiness requires freedom, and freedom will bring happiness only if our free choices are based on knowledge. It is this need for freedom, knowledge, and wisdom that moves the popular conception of happiness toward the philosophical domain. The philosophers will ask: what kind of knowledge do we need for making the choices in life that will lead to happiness and how do we get it?

Outlining these five features of the popular notion of happiness helps us understand what ancient Greeks were calling happiness at the time virtue ethics was developing. Many people today would agree with most if not all of these features. It does seem that the happiness we have in mind when we wish people happiness is a certain kind of life, a life (1) with many goods, (2) that endures over time, (3) that really is a good life (and not merely one that appears good), (4) that satisfies our deepest human desires, and (5) that allows freedom of choice.

The Prephilosophical Definitions of Happiness

The general notion of happiness could be shared by many people because its five major features are rather general, and this generality allows room for different definitions of happiness to develop. And, in fact, several prephilosophical definitions of happiness did emerge among the ancient Greeks. Aristotle lists four of them in his *Rhetoric* (*Rhet.* I, v, 3), an early work very much concerned with how the general public thinks, and then adds a fifth popular definition in the *Nicomachean Ethics* (NE 1095a21–23). The chief prephilosophical definitions of happiness listed in his works are as follows:

1. Happiness is good conduct with virtue (*eupraxia met' aretes*).
2. Happiness is self-sufficiency (*autarkeia*) in life.
3. Happiness is a life of the greatest pleasure with security (hedonism).
4. Happiness is wealth—an abundance of possessions and of slaves with the power to preserve and to use these possessions.
5. Happiness is being recognized and honored as a great person.

Although the virtue ethicists mostly accept the general features of the popular prephilosophical notion of happiness identified above, they do not consider any of the prephilosophical definitions of happiness adequate. Looking at the inadequacies that they found in prephilosophical definitions will enable us to understand more readily their conception of happiness that lies at the heart of virtue ethics.

Transforming the Prephilosophical Definitions of Happiness

The philosophers think that all the prephilosophical definitions of happiness fall short if happiness is to be understood as the overriding good in life.

Happiness Is More than Good Conduct with Virtue

The philosophers acknowledge that happiness includes good conduct with virtue but they consider it more than that. The philosophers insist that happiness designates primarily not good conduct but a good life. Happiness is more than *eu-praxia*—good conduct, good deeds, or good actions. Happiness is *eu-daimonia*—good fate and good fortune throughout a lifetime. Happiness characterizes a whole life. The ultimate good sought in almost all Greek ethics (the Cyrenaics are the exception) is viewed in terms of life as a whole. Good deeds are the way we build a good life but they are the means to the end, not the end itself. In fact, what determines whether or not conduct is good (*eupraxia*) is whether or not it contributes to happiness (*eudaimonia*).

The popular prephilosophical definition of happiness as "good conduct with virtue" (*eupraxia met' aretes*) appears close to a definition of happiness that Aristotle gives at the end of the *Nicomachean Ethics*. According to Aristotle, "happiness is actualization in accord with virtue"(*energia kat' areten*; NE 1177a12; see also 1140b7). However, there are important differences between the two definitions. *Eupraxia* designates good actions or deeds; *energia*, on the other hand, is a technical term denoting the actualization of a being's potential. Thus, Aristotle's *energia* is a much more fundamental term than *eupraxia*. It refers to the fulfillment of a being's total potential and not merely to its actions. This is why Aristotle can say *energia* for human beings includes contemplation (*theoria*), something he sharply distinguishes from action (*praxis*). Aristotle's phrase *energia kat' areten* really means something like "fulfillment of your potential in accord with virtue."

Happiness Is More than Self-Sufficiency

Although the philosophers think that self-sufficiency (*autarchia*) is an important criterion for happiness, they do not define happiness in terms of it. They acknowledge that happiness is self-sufficient (*autarkes*); that is, not in need of anything else, but they do not stop there. They insist that happiness includes other goods. It includes at least the virtues, and both Plato and Aristotle insist that it includes some nonvirtuous goods such as health and pleasure as well.

Happiness Is More than Pleasure

One popular view was and still is that happiness is the same as pleasure. It identifies happiness with feeling good. The philosophers reject this view although most of them think that pleasure plays an important role in virtue and happiness. Plato clearly embraces the value of pleasure in the *Philebus,* as does Aristotle in Books VII and X of the *Nicomachean Ethics.* And even the Stoics, although they decline to make pleasure an integral component of happiness, do acknowledge that it is "preferable" to pain and that the Stoic sage experiences joy in living the virtuous life.

Epicurus would seem to be an exception to the claim that none of the major philosophers define happiness in terms of pleasure; he is widely known as a hedonist who identifies happiness with pleasure. His views, however, are actually more complex than his popular image and they are worth noting. Epicurus distinguishes two kinds of pleasures: *active pleasures* such as drinking water when you are thirsty and *static pleasures* such as the untroubled state you experience when you have quenched your thirst by drinking the water. It is the latter kind of pleasure that he identifies with happiness.

Happiness for an Epicurean is the state of being untroubled—*ataraxia*. Epicurean happiness is pleasure understood as an enduring state of not being troubled, "not feeling physical pain or mental upset" (*Letter to Menoeceus*, cited in Long and Sedley, *The Hellenistic Philosophers*, 2:21B). For Epicurus, the pleasure constituting happiness is not the immediate pleasure derived from engaging in pleasant activities such as eating, drinking, exercising, or sex but the tranquility one experiences when life is functioning well and trouble free, a state that actually requires one to practice great moderation in activities that provide intense pleasure.

The Epicurean state of pleasure or happiness, however, is not simply a passive state of "no trouble." It has a positive side: it is about doing things but doing them in such a way that they bring tranquility and not trouble. Epicurean pleasure is achieved by fulfilling our physical and psychological desires in a way that does not create bodily pain and illness or mental disturbances such as worry and regret. Achieving trouble-free living—what the Epicureans called happiness—presupposes many goods. We need food when we are hungry and peace of mind when we are troubled. And we need, according to the Epicureans, virtue, above all the virtue of prudence. Acting in ways that are intemperate, unjust, imprudent, and cowardly bring trouble, not tranquility. Epicurean philosophy is a hedonism, but it is a hedonism understood in terms of virtue.

Happiness Is More than Wealth

The philosophers consider the identification of happiness with an abundance of possessions and of slaves another popular misconception. They offer several reasons why happiness is not wealth. Happiness is the end sought for its own sake, while wealth is, as Aristotle notes, only a means to an end, not an end in itself (NE 1096a6–10). Moreover, sometimes wealth brings unhappiness and ruined lives. Finally, the philosophers insist that our deliberate choices play a major role in achieving happiness, yet some, those who attain wealth through inheritance, gain wealth without ever choosing it. The philosophers do not think happiness could consist in anything we might achieve solely by luck. We should note, however, that many of the philosophers, most notably Aristotle, insist that some wealth is an integral part of happiness because poverty can ruin one's chances for happiness in life. However, the Stoics, in one of the most intense debates in ancient ethics, disagree. They argue that poverty is no obstacle to happiness, although they concede that wealth is "preferable" to poverty.

Happiness Is Not Recognition and Honor

Another popular view is that happiness—a good life—consists in being honored and recognized as an important person. Honor is a major theme in Greek literature beginning with Homer. The virtue ethicists, however, hold that achieving honor cannot be equated with happiness for at least two reasons. First, a person's happiness should not depend on its being bestowed by other people. They might not recognize that honor is due or they might not bestow it for political reasons. Moreover, once happiness is achieved it should not be easily lost. Yet a person once honored can easily fall out of favor. Hence, although institutions do honor people for their great and virtuous deeds, Aristotle argues that this recognition by others is too unreliable and too superficial to count as happiness (NE 1095b23–1096a4).

We should note, however, that Aristotle found a place for honor among the virtues and hence made it a part of happiness. Aristotle revamped the popular idea of honor, which depended on being recognized by others, so that it became something that the virtuous person recognizes for himself. For Aristotle, it is a virtue for the virtuous person to honor himself for his success in living a truly good life. Authentic virtue is something that a person can be proud of, and the name for this virtuous pride is *megalopsychia*, a word that almost defies translation. Literally, *megalopsychia* means magnanimity, which connotes benevolence, unselfishness, graciousness, generosity, kindness, altruism, and so forth, but none of these meanings really convey how Aristotle used the term to describe the pride a truly virtuous person can rightfully take in the noble life he has created.

The Philosophical Criteria for Happiness

If happiness cannot be defined in terms of good deeds, or self-sufficiency, or pleasure, or wealth, or honors and recognition, then what is it for the philosophers? The philosophers begin their answer by proposing that whatever qualifies for happiness has to meet three important criteria. Happiness will have to be *secure*, it will have to be *complete*, and it will have to be *self-sufficient*. To understand why these criteria are important to the philosophers we need to remind ourselves of a widespread perception about life that prevailed among the ancient Greeks before Socrates emerged. Before the philosophers ancient Greeks felt that fate governed their lives, and fate was often cruel. This view permeates their prephilosophical literature.

Think of how the tragedy of Oedipus haunted Greek culture. Oedipus had it all—honor, wealth, pleasure, power, the woman of his dreams, children, health, prestige, and so forth—but he did not achieve *eudaimonia*, a happy life. Abandoned by his parents, he was saved and raised by loving foster parents. He fell in love with, and was loved by, a recently widowed queen whom he married. He became a king, fathered four healthy children, and was honored and respected by his people. But he lost it all. His father was murdered. His wife hanged herself. He mutilated himself in horror when he realized that his wife was his mother, and he was driven in exile from the city he had helped so much. One of his daughters also hanged herself in prison, and one of his sons killed his brother before dying in combat himself.

Many commentators trace Oedipus's loss of happiness to faults and flaws in his character; Sophocles, however, had a different idea. In *Oedipus at Colonus*, a sequel to *Oedipus Rex*, an old, blind, and dying Oedipus finally sees the truth—the horrible tragedies were not all his fault. He did not know that Laius was his father when he killed him or that Jocasta was his mother when he wed her. Patricide and incest ruined his life and family, yet those tragedies were not really his doing. It was largely fate—bad fate and bad luck—that ruined the happiness of Oedipus.

Bad fate and bad luck are what frightened the Greeks. No matter what we do, no matter how successful we become in life, it can all fall apart. Whether our lives are happy or miserable is a matter of chance—there is nothing we can do about it. If Oedipus's life is a paradigm then happiness and unhappiness are a matter of luck.

The Oedipus story is not the only example of ruined happiness in ancient Greek literature; the sixth century B.C.E. plays performed in the theaters are almost all tragedies. And Homer's magnificent telling of the horrible fate of King Priam of Troy was, as Aristotle notes, another well-known reminder that the happy life of a decent king could go terribly bad. The romantic folly of his son Paris led to a long siege of his city and to the death of another son, the brave Hector, whose body was obscenely dishonored by Achilles. After a long siege, the Greeks sacked Troy, ravaged Priam's family, and put him to the sword.

The historian Herodotus told yet another well-known tragic story. Croesus, the prosperous king of Lydia (a part of modern Turkey), boasted that he was the happiest man alive. Solon warned him that even the happiest of men are vulnerable to disaster. Not long after that warning, the Persians defeated Croesus's armies and took away his wealth and power, leaving his kingdom and his life in shambles.

The philosophers represent a reaction against the idea that happiness depends on luck. Mindful of these tragic stories, they began developing concepts of happiness that would be less vulnerable to the misfortunes typified by the fall of once happy people such as Oedipus, Priam, and Croesus. The thrust of their efforts was to develop a conception of happiness that would be invulnerable, or at least highly resistant, to misfortune and bad luck.

A conception of happiness resistant to misfortune will have to meet the three crucial criteria mentioned above: happiness will have to be *secure, complete,* and *self-sufficient. Security* means that happiness will endure despite misfortune; *completeness* means it will fulfill all our reasonable desires over our lifetime, and *self-sufficiency* means it fulfills these desires without the need of anything else. Although these formal criteria of happiness overlap somewhat, we can consider them separately for the moment.

- *Security.* The major move of the philosophers to make happiness secure is their insistence that it depends far more on how we think and on what we choose to do than on luck and fortune. The philosophers emphasize that we, and not fate, have the primary power to make our lives happy. Happiness arises chiefly from the way we choose to live our lives, and we can position ourselves so that misfortune has little or no impact on our happiness. We achieve it and keep it by learning how to make intelligent decisions and by developing a state of character supportive of good decision making. As we will see, the philosophers make excellence in decision-making and excellence of character the chief sources of happiness.

- *Completeness.* The virtue theorists insist that happiness will satisfy all one's reasonable desires throughout one's entire life. Happiness is thus complete, it is all we need. Upon achieving happiness in our lives, we seek nothing else; happiness satisfies all our reasonable desires. As we will see, Socrates and the Stoics think that happiness is essentially complete once we achieve virtue. Plato and Aristotle, on the other hand, do not think that happiness is complete unless we have other goods in addition to virtue.

- *Self-sufficiency.* Completeness implies self-sufficiency; that is, complete happiness includes whatever it needs. Happiness depends on nothing outside itself for its realization in a particular life. As we will see, making self-sufficiency a criterion of happiness is a challenge because happiness would seem to depend to some extent on other things. But the philosophers insist that it is self-sufficient. Some, Socrates and the Stoics, for example, make happiness self-sufficient by tying it to an inner attitude that remains unaffected by bad luck, tragedy, or even the threat of death. Others, most notably Aristotle, make happiness self-sufficient by including whatever goods are needed for happiness (for example, health and wealth) in the definition of happiness itself.

Security, *completeness*, and *self-sufficiency* are the three formal criteria of happiness for the virtue ethicists. By formal criteria, we mean the standards that any conception of happiness will have to meet. The formal criteria enable us to rule out identifying happiness with pleasure, honors, or money. These things are neither secure, complete, nor self-sufficient. They are vulnerable to misfortune and do not extricate us from the horrors presented in Greek literature from Homer to Sophocles. Of course, the formal criteria of happiness do not tell us much about happiness. For that, we need a rich definition or description; we need to know its defining characteristics. Here, the philosophers appear to let us down because we do not really find a good definition or rich description of happiness in their writings.

Is There a Philosophical Definition of Happiness?

A standard and frequently made critique of ancient virtue theory is that its notion of happiness is too vague and ill-defined to play the normative role they want it to play in their ethics. The critique has considerable merit. Philosophers make the criteria of happiness relatively clear—whatever happiness is it will have to be secure, complete, and self-sufficient, but they really do not give us as clear and comprehensive a definition of happiness as many would like. This may not be oversight. There are several possible reasons why they saw no need or advantage in attempting to define or to describe happiness more thoroughly than they did. First, there was little need to do so because most people already have a general idea of happiness. Happiness (*eudaimonia*) literally and simply means having a good lot in life, having a life that goes well. It is the best anyone can hope for in life. It is the universal aspiration of all peoples.

Second, if the philosophers did develop a precise definition of human happiness it would be counter-productive. Virtue ethics is very much attuned to the particular features of each individual moral agent and each situation where that agent makes decisions. A defining account of what happiness and a happy life are would undermine the sensitivity of their ethics to these particularities. There are many ways for a life to go well, and each person's happiness depends to some extent on the idiosyncratic features of the individual's personality and of the situations in which the agent exists. Happiness has to be a somewhat vague notion because it has to cover many different kinds of life for many different kinds of people living in many different kinds of situations. To describe *a priori* the boundaries of happiness in a strict definition is to close off prematurely the many unknown ways human beings can live truly good lives.

No one can give an exact definition of happiness because each person is unique and lives in a unique set of circumstances. Happiness is living a truly fulfilling and meaningful life, and there are many ways to do this. In fact, one important task in virtue ethics that each individual needs to perform for himself is, as we shall see in the chapters on practical wisdom and prudence, clarifying for himself what counts as meaningful and fulfilling in life. No rich description of happiness can be given in advance because it would not cover all the various good ways the human life of each unique individual can unfold. In many areas of ethics, and this is one of them, we cannot give an exact description. Aristotle acknowledges as much when he says we cannot achieve exactness in matters of ethics (NE 1094b11–27; 1098a26–1098b8; 1103b26–1104a11). Of course, the absence of rich descriptions of happiness by the original virtue ethicists inevitably opens the door to many and varied interpretations as commentators try to explain what the original philosophers meant by happiness. In the past several decades an enormous literature on how the individual philosophers—Socrates, Plato, Aristotle, Epicurus, and the Stoics—understood happiness has arisen as scholars have scoured the ancient texts in an effort to explain how the various philosophers understand happiness. Their differing accounts lead to interesting debates, but unraveling these debates, which often presuppose a knowledge of ancient Greek, will not help us much in this introduction.

For our purposes, we can note that the virtue ethicists emphasize three major defining characteristics of happiness: (1) happiness in life is mostly, perhaps totally, a result of our choices, (2) happiness thus requires deliberation and reasoning so we can make good choices, and (3) happiness also requires good character because only people of good character are able to reason well and make good choices.

Happiness Is Mostly, Perhaps Totally, the Result of Our Choices

Prior to the philosophers, most people, as already noted, tended to think that happiness—having a good life—was mostly a matter of good luck and good fortune, and was relatively rare. The Homeric image of Zeus arbitrarily scattering good and bad fates on mortals was dominant and, of course, upsetting.

The philosophers began changing that view by insisting that happiness is a matter of what we know, how we think, and how we decide to behave. Knowing, thinking, and deciding pertain to what the Greeks called our rational soul. Hence, most, if not all, human happiness will come from behaviors directed by our rational souls. This means that people who can think and are free to choose control in large measure their own fate.

Shifting the cause of happiness from blind fate to human choice explains why Plato and Aristotle do not think that children and many adults in Greek society—slaves and most women, for example—can achieve happiness. These people lack the knowledge and freedom needed to control their fate.

It was relatively easy for Plato and Aristotle to speak of human freedom and choice because they do not postulate a totally deterministic universe; therefore, there is room for human choice in time and history. The Stoics, however, had a problem when they spoke of human choices because the Stoic philosophy of nature is a strict determinism. Everything that happens in the world is completely governed by fate. True, the Stoics believe that the fate governing the world is *Logos* or Reason, which is both rational and beneficial. Nonetheless, everything that happens has been predestined to happen, and this presents a problem for human freedom.

Such determinism would seem to exclude any place for personal freedom in Stoic ethics but, the Stoics claim, it does not. They maintain that freedom lies in our decision to accept or reject our preordained role in this deterministic universe. Choosing to accept the inevitable is precisely the virtuous response that brings happiness. The Stoics do not understand freedom as the ability to have done otherwise than one did. They understand freedom as the decision to accept willingly whatever is destined to happen to us. Wisdom is recognizing that whatever happens is predetermined to happen, that it is for the best, and that our happiness consists in freely embracing this universal plan with joy. We are not free to change history because what happens to us is totally determined. We are free, however, to choose our attitude toward what happens to us, and if we embrace it as reasonable and beneficial we will experience happiness no matter what happens to us.

Both Zeno and Chrysippus, his pupil and his most important successor, illustrate their doctrine of freedom in a deterministic universe with the metaphor of a dog tied to a wagon drawn by larger animals. The dog can choose to follow when the wagon moves or it can choose to resist, but if it resists it will be dragged forward anyway (Hippolytus, *Heresies*, in Long and Sedley, *The Hellenic Philosophers*, 62A). This metaphor show the choices Stoicism offers: we can choose to embrace our destiny willingly, which is the way of happiness, or we can choose to resist our destiny, which is the way of misery because whatever is destined to happen will happen anyway.

This Stoic doctrine of determinism and freedom, of course, raises serious questions about moral responsibility. If freedom is reduced to accepting or resisting a predetermined fate that is destined to happen, if a person cannot do otherwise than what she is destined to do, then her freedom is superficial. If a strong man is about to rape a woman she can certainly choose to submit or to resist, but she is not free to prevent the rape. She cannot choose what really matters. To their credit, the Stoics try mightily to show that people are truly free, and thus responsible for their actions, in a world where everything is determined.

As we have pointed out, happiness, *eudaimonia*, literally means "good fate" in Greek. The philosophers insist that our "good fate" in life is in our own hands more than it is a matter of luck or due to the whim of Zeus. All the important ancient philosophers agree that happiness is mostly, if not totally, dependent on the choices we make in life.

Happiness Requires Knowledge and Reasoning

If happiness is in our hands, we need to know how the world works so we can direct our lives and manage our communities. We need knowledge about the world in which we live, a project already started by the presocratic philosophers such as Thales, Anaximander, Heraclitus, Pythagoras, Parmenides, and others. And we also need knowledge about human psychology; that is, knowledge about human desires, appetites, feelings, and needs. All the early virtue theorists thus pay attention to what came to be called physics, metaphysics, and psychology.

Once we understand something of how the world works and something of human psychology, we need another kind of knowledge—we need to know how to make intelligent decisions in the unpredictable arena of human history where we live with other people. The philosophers also develop some form of practical reasoning for directing human conduct in the complex world of human life, where human freedoms intersect in unpredictable ways. Practical reasoning, and not hoping for good luck, becomes the key for achieving happiness in virtue ethics.

Happiness Requires Moral Character

Making good decisions, those that bring happiness, presupposes a background of good character. People with poor moral character are not likely to make good moral decisions. How does a person acquire the good moral character that supports good moral decision making? The virtue ethicists think that the formation of moral character begins with training and education; it is not something that comes automatically. The training and education begins when parents and other authority figures shape the beliefs of children about right and wrong, and control their actions by encouragement and by punishment. It continues as the customs and rules of society and its institutions further shape the beliefs and influence actions of people as they mature. The goal of this training and education is the formation of a good character by the time the person becomes an adult.

The moral training and education creates good character by instilling the character virtues—virtues such as justice, courage, temperance, piety, and so forth. Strictly speaking, however, these virtues are not yet *authentic* character virtues because the person has not freely chosen them for their own sakes. This pre-ethical stage of good character, however, prepares the person for authentic virtue by orienting him in the right direction.

Authentic virtue and moral character develop when the person begins making his own decisions about how to act and how to live. These decisions gradually coalesce into habits that become enduring states of authentic moral character. Morally reasonable decisions form a good moral character that in turn provides a platform of support for making more and better moral decisions in the future. In other words, good decisions form moral character and moral character improves our ability to make good decisions in the future.

The philosophers thus advance the popular notion of happiness in three important ways. First, they insist that happiness depends entirely or mostly on our decisions; it is not a matter of fate or luck as was commonly thought. Second, they insist that we need knowledge and reasoning if we are to make good decisions; decision making is not a matter simply of making a choice based on a guess or a hunch or a feeling. Third, they insist that we need both moral training and actual decision-making experience if we are to develop the moral character and intellectual expertise necessary for making good decisions.

The expansion of the popular view of happiness to encompass the three ideas of personal responsibility, practical wisdom, and virtuous character leads us to the two major types of virtue in early virtue ethics. Once we see that happiness depends in large measure, if not totally, on the choices we make, then the need for excellence in reasoning to guide our decision making becomes obvious. This excellence in practical reasoning is the intellectual virtue of practical wisdom or prudence. And once we see that good decision making requires the support of good moral character, we see the need for the character virtues. Moral training and education first instills these virtues in pre-ethical form when we are young. Then, when we begin making our own moral decisions as young adults, our decisions form patterns that become the authentic moral virtues forming our good character.

We need the pre-ethical virtues that are created by moral training and education so we can start making good moral decisions on our own, and then these personal decisions develop the authentic character virtues commonly known as the moral virtues with names such as temperance, courage, justice, and so forth. Virtue ethics thus embraces two types of virtue: intellectual virtue and character virtue. Intellectual virtue guides decision making and creates the authentic character virtues in our lives; these, in turn, support our subsequent decision making.

Every ancient philosopher thinks both kinds of virtue—intellectual virtue and character virtue—are the major defining characteristics of happiness. Differences emerge among the philosophers, however, when we investigate the roles that the different virtues play in happiness. Socrates, at least as we find him in Plato's accounts, thinks that the character virtues are little more than variations of the one intellectual virtue that is sufficient for happiness—wisdom. Plato, on the other hand, gives the character virtues distinct identities in the *Republic* and seems to say in that book that both kinds of virtue are sufficient for happiness. Yet in the *Philebus,* he acknowledges that pleasure, which is not a virtue, is also needed for a happy life, thus opening the door for saying that more than virtue is necessary for a good life. Aristotle goes through this door and acknowledges that pleasure as well as other "good things" such as health, financial resources, and stable societies are also components of happiness. Hence, for him, both kinds of virtue are necessary but insufficient for happiness. Epicurus, who identified happiness with pleasure, saw both kinds of virtue not as components of happiness but as the indispensable instruments whereby we achieve the state of pleasurable tranquility that he identified with happiness. Finally, the Stoics take a position close to Socrates: virtue is all we need for happiness and the character virtues are really little more than wisdom in the various domains of life.

Despite these differences, however, the original virtue ethicists all shared a basic conceptual framework. They agreed that the intellectual virtue of practical wisdom or prudence is the key factor in achieving happiness. A person lives a good life only if she is actually managing that life and personally making the decisions that shape it. The defining characteristic of happiness is virtue, and the defining characteristic of authentic moral virtue is intellectual virtue—practical wisdom or prudence.

By aligning happiness closely with virtue, and by insisting that virtue is in the individual's hands, the philosophers reduce tremendously the exposure of happiness to misfortune and tragedy. They make happiness much more secure than it was in the writings of Homer, Herodotus, and the authors of Greek tragedy. Socrates and Plato insist that virtue guarantees happiness, if not in this life than in the next life. After death, as Er's story at the end of the *Republic* reminds us, the virtuous are assured a tenfold reward.

Aristotle is not so sure that virtue guarantees happiness, partly, no doubt, because he does not believe in a personal survival after death. Somewhat reluctantly, it seems, he acknowledges that virtue might not result in happiness because bad luck can ruin a happy life, but he implies that such a failure would be rare indeed. Moreover, as we will see, the virtue theorists also insist that the character virtues are a set of enduring psychological states developed over time. Once in place they are not easily dislodged; therefore, they provide a stable platform for enduring tragedies that threaten happiness. It is no accident that courage and endurance inevitably make the short list of character virtues in so many of the ancient authors.

Epicurus and the Stoics, on the other hand, tend to equate virtue and happiness. Virtue brings happiness without fail. For the Epicurean virtue brings tranquility and peace of mind, the ultimate pleasures of life. For the Stoic virtue brings the joy of knowing that whatever happens is for the best.

In the next chapter, we will look at the character virtues needed for happiness. For the sake of brevity in this introductory text, we will focus on Aristotle's account. Then, in chapters 4, 5, and 6, we will look at the crucial decision-making virtue of practical wisdom first in Socrates and Plato, then in Aristotle, and finally in the Stoics.

Underlying this whole project of studying the ancient ethics is the idea that we increase our chances for happiness by planning our lives around it and by recognizing the crucial role the virtues play in achieving it. Ethics was ever practical for the Greeks. It was a study that mattered personally, and our interest will be piqued if we think of it that way also. Virtue ethics is not predominantly about making general moral judgments; it is about figuring out what personal choices will make our lives good lives.

CHAPTER 3

Character Virtue

Prephilosophical Ideas about Virtue

The word virtue (*arete*) means "excellence" in Greek and it has a long history with many meanings. Some of these historical uses have little to do with what we consider ethics and morality. Homer used the word to describe the fighting spirit of warriors; other authors applied the term to animals and even to things.

By the end of the fifth century B.C.E., one important meaning of excellence designated becoming a good citizen and achieving success in public life, especially in politics and in the judicial system. The Sophists claimed that they could teach people how to achieve excellence in these areas and soon began attracting as students young men who wanted to succeed in Athenian life. The Sophists, in other words, began teaching virtue in Athens.

The leading Sophists, however, did not, indeed most of them could not, practice what they taught because they were not citizens of Athens, an autonomous city-state. Protagoras came from Thrace, a region that once extended over eastern Greece and western Turkey, Prodicus came from an island in the Aegean, and Gorgias came from Sicily. These foreigners became successful in Athens not by becoming good citizens and succeeding in public life, something foreigners could not do, but by charging money for teaching Athenian youth how to achieve the excellence needed to succeed in Athenian life.

As their educational efforts expanded and enjoyed considerable success their teaching also became controversial. Their emphasis on rhetorical skill to win over juries or to persuade people by political speeches regardless of the merits of the cases upset some citizens. Their practice of charging money for teaching virtue also bothered some people, as did the fact that these foreigners had assumed the role of teaching their versions of excellence or virtue in public life to the Athenian youth.

The controversies over their teachings generated considerable discussion about excellence or virtue among the native Athenians, and, toward the end of the fifth century, Socrates became a major player in these ongoing debates. Plato's early dialogues, where we find Socrates' ideas presented, show that the participants found nothing strange about discussing virtue—what it is and how it is acquired. The characters in the dialogues slip easily into conversations about various virtues. In the *Charmides,* the topic is temperance, the *Laches* covers courage, the *Euthyphro* is about piety and justice, and the *Crito* is about justice.

When Socrates and the later philosophers began considering virtue they did the same thing they did with happiness—they began with the prevailing common notions and then challenged and eventually modified them. In the *Protagoras,* for example, the Sophist Protagoras describes virtue as deliberating well (*euboulia*) about one's own affairs and about the affairs of the city as one plays a role in public life (*Prot.* 318E–319A). Socrates then engages Protagoras in interesting discussions about whether virtue can be taught and about whether virtue is one or many and, if there are many virtues, about whether they are separate so that a person might have only some of them.

We can follow the philosophers' approach to virtue first by outlining six major characteristics of the popular or prephilosophical conception of virtue in fifth-century Athens. We can then show how the philosophers modified the characteristics embedded in popular conception and added one of their own. The six major characteristics of the popular conception of virtue are the following.

Virtues Are Admirable and Praiseworthy

The challenge, of course, is determining what virtues are truly admirable. Odysseus, for example, appears as a more admirable character in Homer than he does in Sophocles. In Sophocles' play *Philoctetes,* the clever and wily ways of Odysseus, considered admirable in the Homeric epics, are now presented as faults.

Neoptolemus, the son of Achilles, becomes the admirable character by defying Odysseus once he realizes that Odysseus's plot to kidnap Philoctetes and steal his weapon is riddled with deception and injustice, and is therefore shameful.

Virtues Are Primarily about Actions

Virtue is something someone does. This behavioral view of virtue has roots that go back at least as far as Homer, where the focus was on the deeds of great warriors whose actions received praise because they were heroic and excellent. The idea that virtue was about deeds—deeds that are admirable and not shameful—was very much on the minds of the Athenians in Socrates' day.

Virtues Are Based on Social Roles

The virtues of warriors, for example, would be foolish in the elderly, for example, or in children. Meno, in the dialogue of the same name, begins his discussion of virtue with Socrates by saying that virtue varies with one's role in life (*Meno* 71E–72A). Virtuous behavior is one thing for a man acting as a citizen of the city-state, another thing for a woman living as a wife and homemaker, another thing for children, another thing for the elderly, another thing for warriors, and still another thing for slaves. In other words, virtue is about the actions appropriate to a person's state and role in life.

Virtues Are Disconnected

In the popular conception, each virtue is a discreet entity with no necessary connection to any other virtue. Acting virtuous in one way does not entail acting virtuously in other areas of life. Thus, a warrior might act with great courage in battle but have no temperance or moderation when it comes to wine and sex.

Virtues Can Go against a Person's Best Interests

The honest trader or merchant could see his business collapse in competition with less scrupulous rivals and the courageous soldier could see his health ruined or lose his life when he acts courageously in battle. Neoptolemus put his life on the line when he challenged Odysseus by returning to Philoctetes the awesome bow that the Greeks desperately needed at Troy. Odysseus went for his weapon and Neoptolemus could have lost a terrible fight had not Odysseus decided to back down.

Practical Wisdom or Knowledge Is but One Virtue among Others

Wisdom or knowledge has no special role. It exists as one important form of excellence along with other major forms such as justice, temperance, and courage.

These characteristics of the popular conception of moral virtue were not well thought out or critically examined, nor would we expect them to be. All this changed, however, when Socrates and other philosophers began examining virtue and challenging many of the popular assumptions as well as some of the doctrines of the Sophists. The philosophers soon modified, sometimes radically, the characteristics embedded in the popular notion of virtue and thus began what we know as virtue ethics.

Philosophical Conception of Virtue

The philosophers adapted without modification only the first characteristic of the popular conception; namely, the idea that the virtues are admirable and praiseworthy. They modified the second characteristic and thoroughly revised the last four. In their accounts, the virtues (except wisdom) are not primarily actions but psychological states, they are not ultimately based on our social roles, they are not disconnected, they are never incompatible with our best interests, and practical wisdom is not one virtue among the others but the foundational virtue that creates every other authentic virtue. We will now explore the major characteristics of the philosophers' conceptions of virtue.

Virtues Are Admirable and Praiseworthy

As already noted, this is the one popular characteristic that remained in the philosophical theories.

Most Virtues Are Primarily Psychological States

They refer to our dispositions, habits, and character. Virtues refer primarily to the kind of persons we are, rather than to our actions. The one exception is the virtue of practical wisdom or prudence, which refers mostly to actions. There is a reciprocal relation between character states and actions because our character influences our actions and our actions influence our character. But all the virtues except prudence refer primarily to the character part of this reciprocal relationship. Practical wisdom or prudence, as we will see, is the decision-making virtue that determines what is good for us to do, and what we do creates our character.

Virtues Are Based on Our Humanity

More specifically, virtues are rooted in what the Greeks referred to as the soul. They are not based on our social roles. As Socrates explained to Meno, virtues such as justice or temperance are relevant no matter what role a person occupies in life. What makes us good human beings is a set of virtues that are relevant for everyone regardless of their social position (*Meno* 72C–73C). Social roles certainly shape one's virtues; however, virtues are rooted in the human soul, not in the social roles a person plays.

Virtues Are Connected

If you have one virtue, you have them all. The unity of virtue is a major doctrine of the ancient philosophical theories. Virtues cannot be separated—a person lacking the virtue of temperance also lacks the virtues of justice, love, and so forth. At first, this thesis appears counterintuitive, but once the crucial role of practical wisdom in each and every authentic moral virtue is understood, the unity of the moral virtues emerges as inevitable.

Virtues Are Always in a Person's Best Interests

Virtue never conflicts with a person's self-interest, rightly understood. Again, many find this thesis counterintuitive, which is why much of modern moral philosophy reacts against it by insisting that ethics is about obligation and concern for others, and not self-interest. However, once the ancient theories are well understood, the compatibility of virtue and self-interest will appear inevitable.

Practical Wisdom or Knowledge Is the Foundational Virtue

For Socrates and the Stoics, practical wisdom is really the *only* virtue; for Plato and Aristotle, on the other hand, it is the virtue that creates the other virtues. The character virtues require wisdom to see clearly the most valuable goal in life and to see in each situation what choices will likely move us toward that goal.

As you can see, the philosophers modified most of the characteristics in the popular conception of virtue. In addition, they added an important additional characteristic of their own: Freedom.

Virtue Requires Freedom

A person acquires a virtuous character only by freely choosing for his or her own sake the actions creating those states. Character virtue thus requires personal freedom, the freedom to choose our actions. A person becomes just only by deliberately choosing just actions repeatedly, honest by deliberately choosing honest actions repeatedly, temperate by deliberately choosing temperate actions repeatedly, and so forth. Without the freedom to make personal choices there is no development of the habits and dispositions that constitute the authentic character virtues. Of course, freedom does not guarantee virtue—not every choice a person makes is a choice that helps one live well. Choosing to do something does not mean what is chosen is good.

These seven general characteristics demonstrate how the philosophers' concept of virtue differed sharply from the popular conceptions in fourth-century Athens. As we will see when we explore the nature of virtue in more depth, the Greek philosophical doctrines of virtue are also quite different from most conceptions of virtue found in modern moral philosophy.

To what extent the philosophical conceptions of virtue actually changed the conceptions of virtue in the popular mind is, of course, another question. Although people studied at Plato's Academy, ethics was not their only concern. Aristotle's Macedonian heritage and his relations with Philip of Macedonia and his son Alexander the Great undermined the acceptance of his views in Athens and in other city-states that resented their loss of autonomy in Alexander's empire. Epicurus tried to cultivate virtuous people in his famous "garden," which was a kind of retreat near Athens where people could withdraw and seek a life of wisdom and tranquility, but that approach limited his influence to a select few. Only the Stoics seemed to develop a large following among the general public. Stoic ethics provides a very appealing therapy for coping with the inevitable upsets and tragedies in life, and its influence continued into Roman times and then inspired a number of important themes in Christian ethics as well.

Three Important Distinctions in Virtue Ethics

Three important distinctions made by Aristotle are crucial for understanding his contribution to Greek virtue ethics.

The Distinction between "Character Virtues" (*ethikai aretai*) and "Intellectual Virtues" (*dianoetikai aretai*)

The expression "character virtue" is a translation of "*ethike arete*." Translators frequently translate *ethike arete* as "moral virtue" or "ethical virtue," but these translations fail to convey two significant aspects of *ethike arete*. First, the English adjectives "moral" and "ethical" do not readily convey the notion of "character" as does the Greek adjective *ethikos*, which is from *ethos*, the noun for character. Second, the phrases "moral virtue" and "ethical virtue" are often taken to denote the only virtue that is relevant to what today we call morality or ethics, when in fact the master virtue for morality and ethics in Greek virtue ethics actually is, as we will see, not "moral virtue" or "ethical virtue" but another type of virtue altogether—an intellectual virtue (*dianoetike arete*). In the rest of this book we will translate the singular *ethike arete* as "character virtue" or "character excellence," and the plural *ethikai aretai* as "character virtues."

We need to understand carefully the distinction between character virtue (*ethike arete*) and intellectual virtue (*dianoetike arete*) and how the former is dependent on the latter. Some commentators think of the character virtues as habits. While they are certainly acquired by habituation, they are more than habits. In fact, they are permanent states of character produced by our habits. Thus, Plato says that character grows from habit (*Laws* 792E) and Aristotle echoes the same idea in the *Eudemian Ethics* (EE 1220a39) and in the *Nichomachean Ethics* (NE 1103a17).

A character virtue, then, can be thought of as a state (a *hexis*) created in our psychological lives (our "souls") over time by performing repeatedly certain actions. There is no official list of character virtues—Aristotle identifies more than a dozen—but three of them play a major role in most all versions of Greek ethics: temperance, courage, and justice.

The crucial thing to understand about the character virtues is that they are primarily psychological states created by habitual actions. When the Greek philosophers talk of character virtues—justice or courage, for example—they are usually not talking about just or courageous *actions;* they are talking about character states that they consider just or courageous. Actions can be just or courageous but no action by itself can ever be called an act of justice or of courage simply because it looks like an act of justice or of courage. Actions that look like justice or courage but that are performed for the wrong reason or that are foolish in the circumstances are not really virtuous actions. The person who gives a weapon back to its actual owner out of a sense of "justice" when the owner wants the weapon for immoral purposes is not, according to Plato, acting justly at all. And the soldier foolishly risking his life or resisting the enemy "courageously" because he fears dishonor is not, according to Aristotle, acting courageously at all. For an action to be just or courageous in the virtuous sense, three essential conditions must be met: first, it must arise from the character state called justice or courage; second, it must be reasonable in the circumstances; and third, it must be performed for the right reason.

Mention of "reasonable" brings us to the second kind of virtue in Aristotle's ethics, the one often neglected in modern virtue ethics. Character excellence is not the only excellence we need; we also need "intellectual excellence" (*dianoetike arete*) so we can reason well. Just as character excellence is composed of the character virtues, intellectual excellence is composed of intellectual virtues. Aristotle's major intellectual virtues are understanding (*nous*), science (*episteme*), philosophy (*philosophia*), skill (*techne*), and prudence (*phronesis*).

Aristotle distinguishes two main categories of intellectual virtue: theoretical and practical (NE 1139a5). The major theoretical virtues are science and philosophy; here, the goal is to *affirm* what is factual and *deny* what is not. The practical intellectual virtues are skill (*techne*) and prudence; in this case, the goal is to *pursue* what is good and *avoid* what is not. The practical intellectual virtue of skill pursues good production—the carving of a good statue or the building of a good house. The practical intellectual virtue of prudence pursues good actions—the actions that make our lives good and bring us happiness. Prudence is the practical intellectual virtue relevant to ethics.

One intellectual virtue—understanding (*nous*)—appears in both the theoretical and practical categories. In theoretical thinking, it grasps first principles such as the principle of noncontradiction. In practical thinking, it also grasps first principles—the desire above all for what is good and the morally salient features in each situation. Understanding enables the craftsman to grasp the features of a particular situation relevant to his project of making a good statue or a house and understanding enables a person to grasp the features of a particular situation relevant to his project of achieving happiness (NE 1143a35–b6).

All the ancient philosophers insist to some extent on a set of character virtues and the specific intellectual virtue of practical wisdom or prudence. However, most of the philosophers do not distinguish character virtue and intellectual virtue as clearly as Aristotle does. They often simply enumerate a short list of major virtues that always includes practical wisdom. Socrates emphasizes five major virtues: prudence, justice, courage, temperance, and piety. Plato concentrates on four major virtues: prudence, justice, courage, and temperance. Plato's list of virtues became the standard list of major virtues. They are frequently found in Stoic references and eventually they found their way into Christianity where prudence, justice, fortitude, and temperance are considered the cardinal virtues.

Aristotle's clear distinction between character virtue and intellectual virtue is useful because it enables us to divide the work of the next three chapters. The rest of this chapter will focus on the virtues that constitute our states of character—the virtues such as justice, courage, temperance, and love—and then following chapters will introduce the decision-making intellectual virtue of practical wisdom or prudence.

The Distinction between "Natural Character Virtue" (*arete phusike*) and "Authentic Character Virtue" (*arete kuria*; NE 1144b4–17)

The phrase "character virtue" (or "moral virtue") is somewhat ambiguous because each character virtue (courage, justice, love, and so forth) may exist two ways: it may be a merely *natural* psychological state or it my be a morally *authentic* psychological state. A person's courage or love, for example, may be a natural character virtue (*arete phusike*) or it may be an authentic character virtue (*arete kuria*). The literal meaning of the adjective *kurios* is "valid" or "authoritative." Only the *aretai kuriae*, the authentic character virtues, are those that create human fulfillment and happiness.

Natural character virtues arise from our natural inclinations; furthermore, they may be shaped by some kind of training that directs us to behave in certain ways. Some people, for example, are born with a courageous disposition and others acquire courage thanks to programs that establish courage in a person—military training or self-defense classes, for example. Again, some people are born with a loving and kind disposition and this may be shaped by family experiences and social environments that reward loving and kind behavior, and ignore or punish unloving and unkind behavior. However, the character virtues such as courage or love that arise thanks to natural dispositions and moral training are not the *authentic* or "full" character virtues. Although they have names such as courage or love, they are not the courage and love that make a life truly good. They are, rather, preliminary or premoral character states. They provide an important orientation in our lives when we are young and they also provide some guidance for those adults not mature enough to achieve authentic virtue.

Authentic character virtue does not arise until a person takes charge of her or his life and freely decides to perform the actions that develop the character states known as the character virtues. Unless virtues such as courage and love are the result of actions thoughtfully and freely chosen by the moral agent, they are not *authentic* character virtues. A courageous state is *authentically* virtuous when it is formed by deliberately chosen acts of courage, and the virtue that deliberates and decides what actions to perform, and when, and how, is prudence. Authentic character virtue arises from freely chosen actions directed by prudence: "authentic virtue cannot exist without prudence"(NE 1144b17).

The Distinction between "Good Things" (*ta agatha*) and the Authentic Virtues

A third important distinction in the writings of Aristotle is the distinction between good things and authentic virtues. All the authentic virtues are good things but not all good things are authentic virtues. Good things that are not authentic virtues include health, honor, respect, financial resources, pleasure, and the natural virtues. These nonvirtuous good things are not always good for us because they can be misused and detract from a good life. Even natural virtue can detract from a good life—the natural courage and temperance of a thief, for example, makes him a better thief but not a better person. Authentic character virtue, on the other hand, always enhances a good life.

The philosophers differ on what role the good things that are not authentic virtues play in happiness. Plato and Aristotle claim that some nonvirtuous goods are necessary for happiness. They cannot imagine happiness unless it includes some measure of health, wealth, pleasure, and so forth. Authentic virtue is thus necessary but not sufficient for happiness. The Stoics notoriously disagree and take an extreme position: nonvirtuous goods are not at all necessary for happiness. They do admit that having them is certainly "preferable" to not having them, thus giving them some value, but they are unnecessary for happiness. For that, one needs only authentic virtue. For the Stoics, then, authentic virtue is both necessary and sufficient for happiness. This explains how a Stoic can be stoic in the face of tragedy. As long as a Stoic has authentic virtue, he has happiness regardless of the misfortunes and tragedies haunting his life.

The ancient debates over the role of the goods other than authentic virtue in achieving happiness were intense but need not detain us here. It is enough to note two things. First, the Greeks generally make a distinction between goods that are authentic virtues and goods that are not virtues. And then they acknowledge that some degree of goods other than virtue is either necessary or at least preferable for happiness. Second, they insist that the nonvirtuous things that are good or preferable can be misused and undermine happiness while the authentic character virtues can never be misused. The authentic character virtues are, by definition, the character states that make a life go well.

Nature of the Authentic Character Virtues

The character virtues, as already noted, are psychological states produced over time. They cannot be taught; they are acquired only by actual practice. If the practice originates from a person's natural dispositions, the resulting psychological state is *natural* character virtue. If the practice is dictated by prudence and free choice the resulting psychological state is *authentic* character virtue. We develop authentic character virtue by freely making prudential personal decisions over and over again.

Our deliberate decisions to act reasonably in the various domains of human life congeal into the virtuous states that define our moral character and dispose us to act wisely in these domains in the future. These various psychological states are the authentic character virtues. *Temperance* is the state arising from a history of reasonable decisions about eating, drinking, and sex. *Courage* is the state arising from a history of managing intelligently our feelings of fear, anger, grief, and so forth. *Justice* is the state arising from a history of reasonable decisions about our relations with other people and our participation in building fair institutions and communities. *Love* is the state arising from managing intelligently our relations with intimate others—family, lovers, and close friends.

Authentic character virtues pertain both to the individual and to the social domains of our lives. By the individual domains of life we mean areas of concern where a person's own state of being is foremost. We think of temperance, for example, primarily in individual terms. By the social domains of life we mean the area of concern where other people and the common good are also of major interest. Justice and love are primarily social virtues.

Two words of caution are in order here. First, when we say that the character virtues are "states" this does not imply that the character virtues are passive states. Just as it would be impossible, Aristotle reminds us, to consider a horse excellent if it had the capability of doing well but never left the barn to run well or to carry its rider well or to perform well in battle, so it would be impossible to consider a person excellent (virtuous) if that person had developed the states of being temperate, courageous, just, and loving, but never behaved in such a way (NE 1106a14–24). Although the character virtues are psychological states, they are states concerned with feelings and actions (NE 1106b24). Virtue is a decision-making state, a *hexis proairetike* (NE 1107a1–3), and Aristotle says explicitly that character virtue is a decision-making state (*ethike arete hexis proairetike*, NE 1139a33–34). The states forming character virtue are not passive; rather, they are expressed in what we feel and what we do.

Second, the character virtues need guidance. Left to themselves, they can lead to choices about feelings and actions that are not good for us and that do not enrich our lives with fulfillment and happiness. Brave actions, for example, can be bad for us in certain situations. Loving actions can be bad for us if we are loving the wrong person or in the wrong way or at the wrong time. Even a just action—returning a weapon to its owner who is determined to misuse it, to return to Plato's example—can be bad in some circumstances. The character virtues tend to generate their proper actions—justice generates just actions, courage generates courageous actions, and so forth—but if they are not managed reasonably in each situation, these actions will go astray. Character virtues need the guidance of prudence to avoid the extremes of excess and defect, and to assure that their feelings and actions occur at the right time, about the right things, toward the right people, for the right reason, and in the right way (NE 1106b16–24).

The character virtues depend on the intellectual virtue of prudence in two ways. Prudence first forms the authentic character virtues by directing the decisions that create them. The authentic character virtues occur in our lives only if we deliberately and intentionally choose the actions that create them. Then, once prudence has created the authentic character virtues, it manages them as they generate their proper feelings and actions. There is a kind of rotating causality—prudential decisions create the authentic character virtues; they, in turn, generate their proper actions under the guidance of prudence.

The primacy in virtue ethics thus does not rest with the character virtues but with the intellectual virtue of prudence. The character virtues do not determine what decisions and actions are virtuous in any particular set of circumstances. They are not *a priori* guides for deciding the reasonable course of action; rather, they are the results of prior intelligent decisions. The guide for decision making in virtue ethics is the intellectual virtue of practical wisdom or prudence.

It is important to note this because so many people today speak of the character virtues (justice, love, caring, beneficence, compassion, and so forth) as if they were normative guidelines for making decisions in our lives. They encourage people to act according to justice or love or caring or some other character virtue. This approach to virtue ethics is not what the ancients had in mind. Their character virtues (*ethikai aretai*) are not action-guides operating as moral principles or rules telling us what we ought to do. The decision-making virtue is the intellectual virtue of practical wisdom or prudence, the intellectual virtue that first creates and then guides the authentic character virtues.

Thus, it can be misleading to speak of actions as "just" or "courageous" in virtue ethics. Only one adjective applies to virtuous actions: "reasonable." In Aristotle's ethics, good actions are actions "according to right reason (*kata ton orthon logon*)," and that "right reason" is prudence. Reasonable actions in some circumstances can be called just, in other situations they can be called loving, and in still other circumstances they can be called courageous. But the actions that we call just, loving, or courageous actions are whatever actions are prudent, that is, reasonable, in the situation.

The Number of Character Virtues

How many character virtues are there? There is no set number in the ancient theories. The number of character virtues remains somewhat indefinite because there are as many character virtues as there are ways we can distinguish various domains of human life. Temperance, courage, and justice are the character virtues that receive most of the attention throughout the literature. Socrates also emphasized piety. Aristotle devoted two of the ten books of his *Nicomachean Ethics* to love and friendship (*philia*) and he also made *megalopsychia,* which we will translate as pride, the capstone of the character virtues.

We find several lists of the character virtues in Aristotle and they vary somewhat. In Book I of the *Rhetoric,* Aristotle lists seven character virtues: justice, courage, temperance, magnificence, pride, generosity, and gentleness. The virtue of love is notably absent here, though he does discuss it in Book II of that work. The *Eudemian Ethics* has a list of thirteen character virtues that includes the seven listed in the *Rhetoric* and adds dignity, respect (*aidos*), righteous indignation, sincerity, love, and endurance. The *Nicomachean Ethics* has a rather indefinite listing of the character virtues that includes courage, temperance, justice, love, generosity, magnificence, magnanimity, truthfulness, wit, gentleness, and a few additional virtues for which Aristotle claims there are no names.

While we can name the important character virtues—temperance, courage, and justice, as well as some others such as love, generosity, pride, and truthfulness—Aristotle explains that some character virtues have no name. This is not surprising because any string of deliberate decisions creating a psychological state that makes our lives *good* is a character virtue. Whether we actually name the state created by those decisions is not important. The character virtues are not specific rules or guidelines for action, thus we do not have to specify names for them in advance.

Once we understand that the authentic character virtues are character states generated by repeated intelligent choices in any domain of our lives that we care to distinguish from other domains, we can then see how any list of moral virtues is open-ended and variable. There are many different ways to distinguish different domains in our lives. Inevitably everyone deals with one's appetites for eating, drinking, and sex, so every philosopher speaks of temperance. And everyone deals with fears and difficulties in life, so every philosopher speaks of courage. Everyone also deals with other people, so every philosopher speaks of justice. Beyond these core virtues, the philosophers also speak of various other virtues as Aristotle's lists show. And it would not be out of place for virtue ethicists today to vary the list somewhat, perhaps by adding such virtuous states as caring, tolerance, forgiveness, and so forth.

Pride, the Forgotten Character Virtue

Most people have some familiarity with most of the named character virtues, especially justice, temperance, courage, love, truthfulness, generosity, and so forth. However, one character virtue identified by Aristotle—one that he made the capstone of the character virtues—is routinely neglected in the literature of virtue ethics. This moral virtue is known in Greek as *megalopsychia*. This word is impossible to translate well. One typical translation is "magnanimity," a literal translation of the Latin *magnanimitas*. Magnanimity connotes the idea of a "great soul" (*magna-anima*) and a person with this virtue can be described as "great-souled." Another proposed translation is "dignity." Yet another translation is "pride." Despite the pejorative connotations of the word "pride," this is the word that we will use, following Michael Woods in his translation of the *Eudemian Ethics*, to designate the Aristotelian character virtue *megalopsychia*.

Aristotle tells us that pride is "something like an ordered totality" (*oion kosmos tis*, NE 1123a1). This is another difficult phrase to translate; *kosmos* can mean ornament, honor, and credit as well as an ordered whole. However, from the discussion of pride in Book IV of the *Nicomachean Ethics*, we can gain a little more of what Aristotle means by this character virtue.

The domain of life relevant to pride is that of honor. We honor people for their great deeds; honor is intended as recognition of great personal success. Honor confers prestige and privilege, and the honored person receives the respect and admiration of others. Public signs of honor abound: honorary degrees, testimonials, monuments, memorials, awards, gestures of respect, regalia, gifts, and the like. Honor is an important public good—it is good to honor those who are brave in battle, outstanding in public leadership, generous in contributing to the common good, and so forth.

Of course, public honor is somewhat fickle. The undeserving might receive it while the truly deserving might be overlooked. Moreover, public honor, by its very nature, is unreliable because it depends on others to recognize the achievements. What Aristotle seeks in his virtue of pride is a more reliable form of honor.

To achieve this, he transforms the phenomenon of public honor so that it becomes a major virtue in a good life—the virtue of pride. He does this in two ways. First, he considers achievement of authentic virtue the greatest of great deeds and deems the people achieving virtue worthy of the highest honor. What needs to be honored most is not heroism in battle or brilliant political leadership or great generosity to the community but success in virtuous living. What needs to be honored most is not the life of the warrior or the statesman or the philanthropist but the life of the virtuous person.

Second, he makes the bestowal of honor for success in virtue depend on personal, rather than public, recognition. The virtuous person honors oneself for his or her achievement in living a good life. Private recognition replaces public recognition, self-esteem replaces public esteem, self-respect replaces public respect, self-approval replaces approval by others, self-admiration replaces admiration by others. The person who has achieved the greatest of great deeds—living a truly good life—caps the virtues integral to this life with the ultimate character virtue of pride. The virtuous person had to make many good decisions to become virtuous and is rightfully proud of having succeeded in life.

The basic idea is that a person who has achieved a high level of a truly good life can take pride in accomplishing this, the most important of goals. In fact, taking pride in what we do—being proud and not ashamed of our feelings and behavior—is itself an incentive for living a good life. As the craftsman taking pride in his work is more likely a better craftsman than the one without pride in his work, the person taking pride in what she does and how she treats other people is more likely a better person.

Only our intelligent choices generate the authentic character virtues. If we have developed a virtuous character, it is because we have chosen wisely. Taking pride in our personal achievement is appropriate and it strengthens the other virtuous dispositions in our life. Pride, rightly understood, is the capstone of the authentic character virtues.

Speaking of pride as a moral virtue is not, of course, without concerns. After all, a powerful strain in the Christian religious tradition considers pride a capital sin and proposes an alternative attitude—humility—as an important character virtue. Aristotle sees it differently. Authentic character virtue comes from the choices we make on our own. Being proud of our choices and of our life when it is predominantly a life of virtue is itself an important virtuous attitude because it orders and reinforces the other moral virtues that are making our life a success. When we take pride in our work, we do it better; when we take pride in our lives, we will live them better—and living better is the goal of virtue ethics. It is important, of course, to understand pride rightly. It is not self-conceit or vanity. Pride, rightly understood, is possible only when one is well on the way to creating a successful life; that is, a life characterized by authentic virtue.

The character virtue of pride is especially important when a person needs to confront adversity, misfortune, or personal loss. These unfortunate events hinder the activities necessary for a good life and threaten happiness. Yet a person of excellent character capped by the virtue of pride in living well can better bear the pain and loss well (NE 1100b23–33).

Hence, the character virtue of pride (*megalopsychia*) is "the best" (*kratiste,* EE 1232a35) and the person with this character virtue is also "the best" (*aristos,* NE 1123b27). She or he has achieved significant success in virtue, something that can be done only by making prudent choices repeatedly. The proud person, Aristotle tells us, does good for others but is somewhat uncomfortable when others do good for him or her. The proud person returns more good than that received. Proud people seek approval for their actions, but it is self-approval, not the approval of others. The virtuously proud person considers public recognition and honor of little importance, which is why Aristotle says that some people think the proud person is arrogant or condescending (NE 1124a13–20).

Aristotle's description of pride and of the proud person remains a very controversial part of his work in virtue ethics. Nonetheless, the major features of his idea seem clear. An important domain of human life is our desire for recognition and esteem. Aristotle believes that the achievement most worthy of recognition and esteem is making our lives successful lives—lives of virtue—and that the most important source of recognition and esteem for that achievement is ourselves. Pride and self-esteem, truly deserved, are virtuous components of a life well lived. The proud person takes pride in the right thing—living a truly virtuous life.

The Unity of Virtue

The ancient philosophers insist on some form of unity for the virtues. The virtues are so connected that having one means you have them all. The inextricable unity of all the virtues seems exaggerated. Most of us can easily imagine a person who is deceptive and dishonest in professional life being kind and loving in his or her family life. But the philosophers could not imagine this. For the ancient philosophers, virtue ethics is about living a good life, and life is a unified whole. Therefore, it is natural to think that the virtues, the key elements of a good life, somehow form a unified whole.

Just how virtue forms a unified whole was the subject of a considerable dispute among the philosophers. Looking at some of the major views will give an idea of just how complicated was the debate. There were four major positions.

Virtue Is One Single Reality

There are no *virtues*, just *virtue*, and the name for this virtue is wisdom. The other "virtues" are merely different names for this one virtue. Socrates holds this view and, apparently, so does Zeno, the founder of Stoicism. Socrates' position emerges in the speeches he gave at his famous trial. Charged with violating a specific virtue—piety—he never defends himself by claiming that his teaching was consistent with this specific virtue. His defense rests on claiming that his concern was always to challenge people to care about the one important thing in life which he calls "prudence" (*phronesis*), "truth," "the best state of one's soul," and "virtue." (*Apol.* 29d–30a). Virtue, not the virtues, was Socrates' constant concern (*Apol.* 38a).

Socrates' position emerges more clearly in Plato's *Protagoras*. In this dialogue, Protagoras first claimed that virtue is a single thing but then went on to undermine his position by saying that a person could be courageous but not just, or just but not wise (*Prot.* 329c–e). Protagoras then states that he thinks of virtue as some kind of whole with different "parts" (justice, piety, courage, among others) much as a human face is a whole with different parts (nose, eyes, and so forth). This allows him to say that a person could have some virtues but not all, just as a person could be missing a part of his face, an eye, for example. Thus a person might be courageous but not temperate or just.

It becomes clear as the dialogue unfolds that Socrates believes that the unity of virtue is stronger than a unity of a whole with disparate parts. He holds instead that the many virtues we speak of are simply different names for one and the same thing. Socrates argues that the different virtues entail each other: justice is pious and piety is just (*Prot.* 331b). Toward the end of the dialogue he takes a more radical position: all the character virtues—he explicitly mentions justice, temperance, and courage—could not be anything else but one thing, and that one thing is knowledge. The context makes it clear that by knowledge he means the wisdom to choose wisely in the various situations we confront in life (*Prot.* 360d–361b). This central role of wisdom is confirmed in another dialogue, the *Euthydemus*, where Socrates claims that wisdom is the one single thing (*monos*) that makes a person happy and fortunate (*Euthyd.* 282c–d).

The Socratic aphorism "virtue is knowledge" is widely known but his position would be better stated as "virtue is wisdom." Wisdom is the knowledge of what is good or bad for me, and it is the only virtue there is. There are not several virtues but one, and the one virtue is practical wisdom. Temperance, courage, justice, piety, and wisdom are, according to Socrates, five different names for the same thing.

Zeno's position echoes that of Socrates and is reported in a well-known passage by Plutarch (who lived much later, from 45 to 120) as follows: "Zeno of Citium . . . defines prudence in matters of distribution as justice, prudence in matters of desire as temperance, and prudence in matters of standing firm as courage" (*Moralia*, 441a).

Some scholars wonder whether Zeno actually embraced the Socratic position and advocated a single virtue—prudence or wisdom. One reason for their concern is another passage from Plutarch where he tells us that Zeno also speaks of several different virtues as did Plato, and thus contradicts himself (*Moralia*, 1034c). Zeno is important because he is the founder of Stoicism; unfortunately, exactly what he held about the unity of the virtues will probably never be known as little of his work survives. Most of what we know of his doctrines is by way of commentators, and they are not always friendly commentators. We do know, however, that the Stoics describe the virtuous person in Stoicism not as the just person, nor as the loving person, nor as the courageous person, but as the *wise* person, the *sophos*.

Virtue Is One Single Reality with Many Different Manifestations

Virtue is one reality—wisdom—but gives rise to different virtuous qualities. A virtuous person has a whole host of qualities such as bravery, justice, gentleness, gracefulness, and so forth. The Stoic Chrysippus (c. 280–207 B.C.E.), the third leader of Stoicism after Zeno and Cleanthes, holds this view. Plutarch reports disparagingly (he was not a fan of Stoicism) that Chrysippus thus introduced a "beehive of virtues" (*smenos areton—smenos* is the Greek word for beehive!) in virtue ethics (*Moralia* 441b).

Chrysippus's view, and not Zeno's, is actually more typical among the later Stoic philosophers. There could be two reasons for this. First, we have a natural tendency to distinguish the various virtues (we differentiate between justice and temperance, for example), and, second, Chrysippus probably had good reason for saying that his way of understanding the unity of virtue was what Zeno really had in mind. Perhaps Zeno did think this way despite the first text we quoted; sadly, we can never know for sure.

Virtue Is a Complex of Individual Virtues United by Justice

This is Plato's view as expressed in the *Republic*. After proposing his famous city-state with three classes—the providers of life's necessities, the guardians, and the rulers—he describes justice as the proper integration of these three classes so they form a viable political unity. Then he describes the human soul in analogous terms. It also has three parts—an appetitive part, a spirited part, and a rational part. The different parts of the soul enable us to speak of different virtues: temperance for appetitive desires of hunger and thirst (*Rep.* 432c), courage for spirited desires such as anger and fear (*Rep.* 429b–c), and wisdom for the rational desire to achieve happiness in life as a whole. And uniting these parts of the soul so they are integrated and function well as a whole is, as it was in the city, the virtue of justice (*Rep.* 441e). The virtues are many but each one implies the others and they form a functioning unity thanks to justice. As we will see, however, the controlling virtue in Plato remains prudence and the schema of the *Republic* faded from his concerns in such later works as *Philebus*, *Statesman*, and *Laws*.

Virtue Is a Complex of Individual Virtues United by Prudence

This is Aristotle's view. The two major categories of virtue—character virtue and intellectual virtue—correspond to the major division in the soul between its two major parts—the nonrational and the rational. The nonrational part of the soul becomes authentically virtuous when it is guided and cultivated by the rational part. The nonrational part comprises various appetites, emotions, and feelings so we can speak of various moral virtues such as temperance, love, generosity, courage, justice, and so forth. The rational part also comprises various kinds of rationality but the one relevant to ethics is prudence.

Despite the plurality of virtues Aristotle agrees with Plato that they are inseparable—if you have one you have them all. However, justice is not, as it was for Plato in the *Republic*, the unifying virtue. Prudence plays this role in Aristotle: "As soon as the one virtue of prudence arises all the virtues come into being" (NE 1145a1–2). However, Aristotle, unlike Socrates, does not identify virtue with wisdom or prudence. Other virtues besides prudence—the states known as the character virtues—are needed to live a truly good life, a life of happiness. Prudence, the virtue of the intellect, is not the only virtue. It generates the other virtues, the nonintellectual virtues that comprise our character.

After Aristotle, the Stoics tend to revert back to a position close to Socrates as we have already noted. Many of their texts speak of the character virtues as if they were several or many in number, as Chrysippus certainly did, but, in the end, wisdom is the one master virtue in Stoicism. What becomes in Stoicism of the appetitive and spirited parts of the soul that Plato and Aristotle identified? These parts of the soul exist according to the Stoics—people certainly have appetites and emotions—but the Stoic idea is that reason should not try to cultivate and guide them, as Plato and Aristotle recommend, but root them out! The Stoic *sophos* does not try to cultivate the appetitive drives and emotions. They are not natural tendencies that can be shaped; rather, they are weeds that must be rooted out—extirpated. The extirpation of the passions and emotions is a major characteristic of Stoic ethics.

One unavoidable conclusion that emerges from a consideration of authentic character virtue in ancient virtue ethics now clearly emerges—practical wisdom or prudence plays the central role in ethics. Prudence, which ironically is not one of the character virtues, the *ethikai arete*, is nonetheless the indispensable and foundational virtue for ethics. The next chapter will summarize how Socrates and Plato understood this key virtue, and then subsequent chapters will consider the views of Aristotle and the Stoics.

PART TWO

Prudence and Character Virtue

The emphasis in virtue ethics today centers on the character virtues such as justice, love, care, compassion, kindness, courage, truthfulness, temperance, and so forth. Often neglected or reduced to secondary status is the foundational virtue of Greek virtue ethics—the intellectual virtue of practical wisdom or prudence. Yet, no one becomes truly virtuous or lives a good life without a personal history of making good decisions, and prudence is the virtue of decision making.

The emphasis on decision making and its virtue, practical wisdom or prudence, means that ancient virtue ethics is strongly intellectual and personal. Although rooted in desire and concerned with feelings and emotions, its primary activity is a form of practical reasoning whereby each person actually deliberates and then chooses what makes his or her life a good life. The rational soul is the distinguishing feature of human nature, and people are most human when they personally engage in the thinking that leads to rational and intelligent behavior. Virtue ethics is about making intelligent decisions. Making a decision means that we are going to do or not do something and that we will have to live with the consequences. The reasoning used in decision making is *practical* reasoning—we find ourselves in the middle of things and we need to figure out what action will achieve our goal of living well. The following chapters offer an introductory explanation of the various ways the original ethicists understood this practical reasoning.

We will look at four major versions of practical wisdom or prudence: the Socratic, the Platonic, the Aristotelian, and the Stoic. As we have already noted, the words for this decision-making virtue in the ancient texts are *sophia* and *phronesis*. Great care is needed in translating these words because some Greek philosophers use them to mean both theoretical wisdom, which is contemplating the nature of things, and practical wisdom, which is deciding what to do to achieve happiness. While Aristotle made an effort to define the terms by reserving *sophia* for theoretical wisdom and *phronesis* for practical wisdom, other authors are not so careful. Plato, for example, sometimes uses *sophia* to mean practical wisdom about deciding what to do and sometimes to mean theoretical wisdom giving us knowledge of the eternal Forms. And he sometimes uses *phronesis* to mean knowledge of the Forms, although he uses it more often to mean wisdom about deciding what to do in a given situation.

In the next three chapters, we will translate the Greek word *sophia* in the usual way—as wisdom. The wisdom of concern in ethics, however, is practical wisdom; that is, wisdom as it relates to making decisions about what to do, and not wisdom understood as understanding reality in a theoretical or contemplative way. We will thus translate *sophia* as practical wisdom whenever the context makes it clear that it is the wisdom engaged in deciding what to do. And we will usually translate *phronesis* as prudence, although we will sometimes leave it untranslated so you can better grasp the uniqueness of the term.

It is becoming more common to see the word *phronesis* in contemporary ethical literature, especially the literature of virtue ethics. However, the modern uses of this word are often misleading. Its appearance in discussions of virtue ethics suggests that the original Greek meaning is being revived but usually this is not the case. In contemporary literature *phronesis,* or "prudence" and "practical wisdom," usually connotes a kind of fine tuning that brings sensitivity and flexibility to various forms of law-based or principle-based ethics. *Phronesis* is understood as a kind of wisdom that sees when exceptions should be made to principles and rules, or that applies principles and rules with discretion, or that notes extenuating circumstances in casuistic ethics, or that mediates between principles and rules when they conflict. *Phronesis* has none of these meanings in Plato, Aristotle, or the Stoics, and the use in modern texts of the actual Greek word but with new meanings misleads readers who are not familiar with the original meaning. We need to remember that the word *phronesis* in ancient virtue ethics denotes a far more fundamental and richer concept than the usual meanings of "prudence" or "practical wisdom" today.

The Greeks would consider the modern language of moral principles (or moral laws, rules, and rights) a distraction from seeing how virtuous people actually manage to live good lives. Prudence, not principle, is fundamental. Practicing prudence is what the virtuous person does, and should do, because prudence is the only way that he can realize the goal and vision of living a good life in an ever-changing world. Principles (and moral laws, rules, and rights) are important but prudence does not follow principles; principles follow prudence.

CHAPTER 4

Prudence in Socrates and Plato

Wisdom and Prudence in the Socratic Dialogues

We will now consider the virtue of wisdom as it emerges from Socrates' teachings and Plato's writings. The views of Socrates and Plato vary considerably; just how great the divide is difficult to determine because we are dependent mostly on Plato to convey his mentor's views. It is difficult to determine just when Plato is reporting what Socrates said and when he is using Socrates to express his own views. In general, scholars think that the Socrates presented in the early dialogues—the "Socratic" dialogues—is speaking mostly for himself, while the Socrates speaking in the later dialogues is speaking mostly for Plato. We will follow that general view, and also add some comments from Xenophon, who knew Socrates and reports some controversial comments about him.

Unlike Plato and Aristotle, Socrates described the soul as totally rational. It has no irrational "parts." It has appetites and desires, but they are ultimately cognitive in nature—if I am thirsty, I crave a drink not because I am thirsty but because I *know* or at least I *believe* that the water will give me satisfaction. If the soul is totally rational, its excellence will consist in intellectual virtue alone—knowledge, wisdom, prudence, and so forth.

After claiming in the *Euthydemus* that happiness is the overriding goal in life, Socrates considers a preliminary list of what goods are needed for a life to be happy. Happiness will apparently require such good things as (1) financial resources, (2) physical advantages (health and attractiveness), (3) status in the community based on birth, power, and honor, (4) good fortune, (5) temperance, justice, and courage, and (6) wisdom (*Euthyd.* 279A–C). The Athenian public had already assumed that some or all of the first five goods are necessary for happiness. Socrates disagrees with the common assumptions. The goods listed in the first four categories are not needed for happiness and, as we saw in the last chapter, the character virtues listed in the fifth category are merely different names for wisdom. Hence the startling thesis of Socrates: The only thing a person needs for achieving happiness in life is wisdom.

Wisdom alone secures and guarantees happiness. How can Socrates say this? How does he think that the exercise of wisdom alone is enough to make a person happy? His answer rests on his conception of wisdom. The truly wise person knows that all the so-called goods (money, health, honor, and so forth) are really not essential ingredients of happiness. If you have them, you still might not achieve happiness; some wealthy, healthy, and much honored people are not happy. These goods do not by themselves bring happiness; they bring happiness only if managed wisely. Having the goods is not enough; you need wisdom to use them well. And if you do not have these goods? Then you need the wisdom to give up your desires for these goods, something you can do once you convince yourself that virtue is the only good you really need for happiness. Living well requires only wisdom—the wisdom to use well the goods you might have or to adapt your desires so you do not become unhappy without the goods you might not have. Wisdom, and by implication the character virtues with which it is identified, is sufficient for happiness although the other goods can enrich that happiness.

Once I develop this wisdom, even the threat of execution, as Socrates shows so well in his speeches before the Athenian court and in the death scene recorded by Plato in the *Phaedo*, will not undermine my happiness. If need be, I can let go of everything, even life itself, and still have happiness if I attribute happiness to the virtue of wisdom. In a sense, I make my own "good fate." With the wisdom that shows us that we can be happy without any of the "goods" other than virtue, we can live (and die) happily no matter what happens to us. Upon realizing that we do not need anything else for happiness but the personal integrity that comes from wisdom, no loss of anything else will make us unhappy.

Although Socrates does not elaborate on how this wisdom guides us in making good decisions, hints are scattered through the early works of Plato. In the *Apology*, for example, he admits someone could say that his habit of challenging so many powerful people in Athens was not wise but foolish because it resulted in his arrest and could lead to his execution. But he argues that his decision to challenge the Athenians was sound because he thought it was best to wake up the Athenians from their unexamined lives. Reminding his audience that he had carried out the orders of his commanders despite great danger when he served in the military, he insists, "Whenever a man takes a position he thinks is best or is put there by his commander, there he must remain not taking into account death or any other thing more than shame" (*Apol.* 28D).

Once a person believes that the best way to live is by engaging in a provocative philosophical enterprise of critical thinking then, Socrates argues, deserting that work for any reason, even the threat of death, would be shameful. Wisdom guides our decisions by first setting as our goal what we think is *best*—for Socrates this was a life devoted to encouraging virtue or wisdom—and then dictates the actions compatible with this goal. Nothing, not even fear of death, can deter us from the goal set by knowledge and wisdom.

But just how does Socrates think that the decision-making virtue of wisdom works in practice? How do we actually make virtuous decisions? It is not easy to say because practical reasoning is a complicated process embracing experience, insight, intuition, imagination, analogy, metaphor, narrative, interpretation, and dialogue that cannot be distilled into a method or some kind of decision tree. Yet one ancient text—the *Crito*—provides a dramatic account of Socratic decision making.

In the *Crito*, Socrates is on death row awaiting execution and a man named Crito visits him with a plan for his escape. Crito and other supporters of Socrates have the money to free him and get him out of Athens. Crito encourages Socrates to escape with all sorts of arguments. He reminds him that his friends have the money, that they are willing to take the risk of being punished if they are caught, that it will not require a lot of money, that he (Crito) will lose a dear friend if Socrates dies, that the execution will leave Socrates' children without a father, that the case never should have come to court, that the trial was poorly conducted, and finally that Socrates' supporters will think it is cowardice, and thus evil, shameful, and not virtuous, for them and for Socrates himself to allow the execution to proceed when they could prevent it. Crito begs Socrates to consider all this and urges him to accept the offer of escape (*Crit.* 44B–46A).

Socrates first reminds Crito that he always makes decisions by relying on reason (*logos*) and on what appears best according to his reasoning, and that his staying or escaping will depend on which alternative is more reasonable (*Crit.* 46B). He then reminds Crito that his claim that people will think he and his friends are cowards if they dare not arrange an escape after such a botched trial misses the point (*Crit.* 46A). We ought not to pay attention to the opinions of all people but only to those of prudent people (the *phronimoi*); that is, to the people who have developed the virtue of *phronesis* or prudence (*Crit.* 46A, 47A). An athlete does not listen to the fans but to the coach (*Crit.* 47B). Most opinions held by others are not important; the only opinions that count are those advanced by those who understand the matter at hand (*Crit.* 48A).

The text then narrates Socrates's deliberation and decision making. He first frames the moral issue: What is of the greatest importance to a person is not living (*zen*) but living well (*eu zen*), and living well is the same as living nobly (*kalos*) and living rightly (*dikaios*) (*Crit.* 48C). The goal, then, is not life but a good life. And the issue for Socrates is whether or not escaping will make his future life a good life.

The main points in Socrates's deliberation then unfold. He argues that he should not seize the opportunity to escape for the following reasons: the city of Athens has given him much so he should not leave it; flouting the justice system will harm the city; the city's judicial system is important and should not be undermined; he would have accepted the jury's verdict if he was found innocent; one cannot pick and choose the laws and verdicts he will respect; it is always better to suffer a wrong than respond to a wrong with another wrong; those who help him escape will be exposed to difficulties with the authorities; he will not flourish in any other city because it will be known that he is an escaped convict; his questionable reputation will hinder his attempts to teach virtue in his new city; if he escapes he will either have to abandon his children or uproot them and take them with him into exile; if he is executed his children will be cared for by his friends; and he will not be well received in the next life if he escapes because he will have returned evil for evil (*Crit.* 48C–53C).

In other words, Socrates reasons that escaping will not bring him happiness and a good life. He, in fact, has no desire for life unless it can be a good life. He argues that he better achieves his goal of living a good life by submitting to the execution than by allowing his friends to buy him out of jail and set him up in exile. Reason, not fear of death, is what drives his decision. He concludes that escaping is immoral because it will not bring him a good life and living well—not merely living—is the whole point of virtue ethics.

That is how Socrates made his decision not to escape, at least in the narrative Plato gives us. It does not matter whether we think his decision is reasonable or not. The point is that he deliberated carefully and became convinced that it was the reasonable thing for him to do, and this is what counts in virtue ethics. Could he, given his personal life history and the things he said in his speeches before the Athenian court, argue that escaping would lead to a good life—a noble and admirable life? It is difficult to see how he could have. Could another person, given her personal life history, argue that escaping a legal but unjust execution would lead to a good life—a noble and admirable life? Possibly. Virtue ethics is very sensitive to the particularities of the person making the decision—one's life story, relationships, and myriad other personal circumstances.

The important point for our purposes is to see how Socrates, and all the virtue ethicists, make decisions—they focus on the overriding goal (happiness, living well, living virtuously) and then deliberate and reason. They weigh the pros and cons, the advantages and disadvantages, all the while keeping in mind the overriding goal—not simply living but living a good life.

The *Crito* is a special text because it depicts in detail a man committed to living a good life deliberating in a life-and-death matter. It provides a valuable glimpse into how practical wisdom and prudence lead to moral decision making. But it leaves numerous questions in our minds. What does Socrates mean when he says in the last line of the text that "god" (*o theos*) is guiding him (*Crit.* 54e)? It probably should be understood to mean not that God gives directions but that God encourages people to follow the directions of their reason as Socrates is doing. And how coherent is it for Socrates to say that he does not consider his children but only what is "right" when he makes this decision (*Crit.* 54b)? Many parents would think that what will happen to their children, especially if they are young, is a significant factor in determining what is "right." And Socrates manifests no concern for Crito's argument that his death will take from Crito a dear and irreplaceable friend (*Crit.* 44B).

Perhaps even more disturbing is the undesirable outcome of what Socrates called wisdom and virtue. In the *Phaedo*, a dialogue that describes the execution of Socrates, Plato has Socrates say that "the only true standard" (*monon to nomisma orthon*) for making choices is prudence (*phronesis*, *Phaed.* 69A). If death row is where prudence (virtue) takes us, then most people will look elsewhere for managing their lives. And there is something counterintuitive about the way Socrates "cheerfully" drinks the hemlock (*Phaed.* 117C). Years later, Aristotle described a more understandable attitude in the face of death: a virtuous person facing death is full of regret, not cheer, because it is the end of a good life.

Xenophon's Account of Socrates' Deliberations

The reasoning presented by Plato in the works surrounding Socrates' death—the *Apology*, the *Crito*, and the *Phaedo*, might not tell the whole story. Xenophon, a student of Socrates who was away on a military campaign when Socrates was executed, also wrote about Socrates' thinking as he approached his death. He apparently interviewed Hermogenes, who knew Socrates well and was present at the execution. According to Xenophon, Hermogenes gives a quite different account of Socrates' reasoning. He reports that Socrates told him that he had received some kind of divine sign that this was the time for him to die, that he was nearing the end of his life (he was about seventy at the time, which was well beyond the average lifespan in that era), that death by hemlock was better than facing the decline of his mental and physical powers as well as the possibility of a painful illness, and that such a death would spare his family the burdens of his old age and final illness (*Memo.* 4.8.6–8).

Xenophon's account of Socrates' deliberations is much less idealistic than what we find in Plato's works. In Xenophon, we see a seventy-year-old man weighing the pros and cons of drinking hemlock, and finding that death at this stage of his life and in these circumstances might be more reasonable than acquittal followed by inevitable decline into old age, illness, and death. Indeed, many of the Stoics, who took much from Socrates, advocated suicide at the end of life as a more reasonable death than enduring senility and suffering. The problem, of course, is that many philosophers—Bertrand Russell among them (in his *History of Western Philosophy*)—disparage Xenophon's account, arguing that he was not a philosopher and could hardly understand the philosophical arguments that Plato puts in Socrates' mouth.

Perhaps that is so, but other scholars disagree. Xenophon, who knew Socrates well, was not a stupid man. According to Gregory Vlastos, he displayed "shrewd judgment of the world and of men" (*Socrates*, p. 101). Moreover, the claim that Hermogenes and Xenophon misunderstood Socrates' prudential reasoning and just "didn't get it" undermines what Socrates thought he could do. Socrates insists that ethics is a practical enterprise that many can grasp. He spent much of his life helping people—and not just philosophers—reason well about living well.

Xenophon was no fool. If he misunderstood Socrates' reasoning, so, then, would most nonphilosophers, and this would confine an understanding of Socratic ethical reasoning to an elite few—the philosophers or the Bertrand Russells of this world. Actually, as we will see in the next section, this is exactly what Plato does in the *Republic,* where he advocates an elite class of philosophers whose knowledge and wisdom direct the lives of the rest of the people in the city-state. This elitism, however, does not appear in earlier Socratic dialogues, where Socrates is depicted teaching all kinds of people, especially the young, about the wisdom needed to make intelligent decisions about living. And in dialogues written after the *Republic*, Plato de-emphasizes the moral authority of a philosophical elite. In his last work, the *Laws*, he advocates a public education system that will teach ordinary citizens how to make the intelligent decisions that will lead to authentic virtue and happiness.

Prudence in the *Republic*

By the time Plato comes to write the *Republic,* he is rejecting several important Socratic ideas. He rejects the Socratic idea that a person will always do what he or she thinks is good. Socrates had claimed that virtue is knowledge—once you know what is good, you will do it. Immorality is *always* ignorance. It is never the result of weakness (you know what is good for you but you fail to do it) or of deliberate self-destructive behavior (you deliberately do what you know is not good for you). Plato disagrees with this. Sometimes we know what is good for us but we do not do it because our appetites or feelings lead us to make a different choice.

Plato also rejects the Socratic doctrine that virtue is a single reality. Socrates claimed that the soul has only one quality—rationality—and thus needs only one virtue—wisdom. Plato disagrees and, as we have already pointed out, claims the soul has three "parts"—the appetitive, the spirited, and the rational—and each part needs its proper virtue. The appetitive part needs temperance, the spirited part needs courage, the rational part needs wisdom, and the unity of the various parts with due recognition to each requires justice.

What Plato did not reject, however, was Socrates' insistence that virtue and a good life can be achieved only by people who manage their own lives. In Book I of the *Republic,* Plato presents a kind of "function" argument. In short: Things have functions, and if they function well they manifest their proper virtue or excellence. If a horse functions well it has its proper excellence or virtue, if a knife cuts well it has its virtue, and if our eyes see well they have their proper virtue (*Rep.* 352E–353C). Plato's interest, of course, is not horses or knives or eyes, but the human soul. To know its virtue we must know its function. And what is the soul's function?

Plato's answer goes to the heart of virtue ethics: the function of the soul is to *deliberate* (*bouleusthai*), to manage (*epimeleisthai*), and to rule (*archein*). Unless a person's soul manages, deliberates, and rules, his soul is not functioning well and he is not living a good and virtuous life (*Rep.* 353D). The goal of moral education is to train, educate, and habituate people so they come to the point where they personally deliberate and manage their own lives, where they rule themselves. The function of the soul is not to be managed but to manage, not to be ruled but to rule, and not to apply moral principles but to deliberate. Reduce moral reasoning to applying principles and rules, as does so much of modern ethics, and you destroy the ability of the soul to become virtuous. A soul cannot become virtuous unless it actually performs its functions of deliberating, managing, and ruling; if these are suppressed in the name of obeying moral authorities or following moral laws, principles, or rules, the soul is not functioning properly and cannot achieve its excellence.

Plato does not believe, at least in the *Republic*, that many people can actually get to the point where their souls could function well enough to deliberate, manage, and rule their lives successfully. Most people need the guidance of those who have achieved virtue—the philosopher-rulers. For those unable or unwilling to deliberate, manage, and rule their own lives, following the wisdom of those who have succeeded in managing their lives is the next best thing. But living a life managed and ruled by others is not yet living a fully functioning human life because the person's own soul is not yet functioning well. It is the best most people can do but it is not yet authentic virtue and the life so lived is not yet a life of happiness.

So the soul, specifically its rational part, deliberates, manages, and rules the virtuous person. The verb Plato used for "ruling" in these sections is *archein*, a very strong verb in Greek, and it tells us a lot about what reason does in virtue ethics. The *arche* of anything is its beginning, its first cause or foundation; you cannot go beyond the *arche* of something. *Arche* also means supreme power and sovereignty. Hence the verb *archein,* which means to rule with supreme power. When Plato uses *archein* in explanations of what the rational part of the soul does it conveys the idea that the activity of the rational soul is the foundation of virtue ethics. In other words, wisdom or prudence rules.

The virtues of the nonrational parts of the soul, virtues such as temperance, courage, and justice, are not the ruling virtues. These virtues do not tell us what to do when we are making a decision. The guide for action in Plato's virtue ethics is neither justice, nor courage, nor temperance, nor any other moral virtue; it is wisdom or prudence. Plato, then, agrees with Socrates that wisdom and knowledge are not only necessary for virtue; they are the very foundation of virtue.

The first book of the *Republic* provides an important clue showing how wisdom and not any of the character virtues, not even the important character virtue of justice, is the ruling virtue for ethical decision making. Polemarchus suggests that justice is giving each person his due, a rather standard and traditional description of the virtue. Socrates immediately shows how justice, so understood, is not always virtuous and good. Suppose, for example, you borrow weapons from a friend and agree to return them whenever your friend asks for them. Obviously, justice indicates that you should return them when asked. After all, they are your friend's property and you promised to return them. But when he comes to retrieve them you notice that your friend is drunk. Now what do you do? Do you let justice be your guide and return the property? Or do you let prudence be your guide and refuse your friend's request? The implication is clear; prudence and not justice is the guide for making this ethical decision (*Rep.* 331C–D).

By the time of writing the *Republic*, however, Plato is moving away from the Socratic position that wisdom or knowledge is the only thing we need for virtue. In the *Republic,* Plato insists that we also have to train the nonrational parts of the soul or they will not always respond to wisdom. In other words, wisdom makes us virtuous but it cannot do it alone. Wisdom needs the support of temperate appetites (temperance), of courageous feelings (courage), and of a fair balance of the appetitive, spirited, and rational parts of the soul (justice). Thus, for Plato, there is not one cardinal virtue as there was for Socrates; rather, there are four: temperance, courage, justice, and wisdom.

Although Plato consistently lists the four cardinal virtues together, they are not at all similar in type. Three of them—temperance, courage, and justice—pertain to a person's character. These first exist in a premoral state as natural tendencies, which can be developed by training and education. They are not truly virtues, however, until they are directed by the fourth cardinal virtue—practical wisdom or prudence.

True virtue begins only when the young person actually begins practicing wisdom; that is, begins deliberating and ruling her or his life. Just as the *Republic* envisions a state whose elite guardians have the wisdom to grasp the essence of things and then rule the other parts of society (the assistants and the workers), it also envisions a moral agent whose rational soul has the wisdom to rule the other parts of the soul. The ruling reality in both the city and the individual remains wisdom—the wisdom of the elite guardians for the city and the wisdom of the individual for himself. However, just as a city-state needs more than the ruling guardians to be successful—it needs the other two classes as well –a good soul needs more than its rational part to be virtuous—it needs the other well-managed parts of the soul (the appetites and feelings) as well.

The comparison of the soul with its ruling part to the city with its rulers is strong in Book IV of the *Republic* (*Rep.* 441C–443B) and it suggests a tension in Plato's ethics. To Plato, people achieve authentic virtue only by ruling themselves by the wisdom of their own souls; however, the task of the elite guardians is to rule the people in the two lower classes. To the extent that the two lower classes are ruled by the elite, they are not ruling themselves; thus, they are not achieving authentic virtue. Plato is careful to point out that behaving rightly "on the outside" (*exo*) and following the rule of others is not enough for virtue; virtuous behavior originates "on the inside" (*entos*) of the person (*Rep.* 443D).

Hence the tension: It is crucial in the city state that the elite philosopher-rulers rule and the rest follow, but those following the rulers, despite performing good actions, do not thereby become virtuous and achieve *eudaimonia*. Happiness is living well, and a human being is not living well unless her own soul is deliberating and ruling her life. Authentic virtue has to be personal, it has to proceed from the inner personal core of each person. A person does not become virtuous by conforming to the will or legislation of another but by ruling oneself and setting one's own life in order, thereby becoming a friend to him- or herself (*Rep.* 443C–D).

Toward the end of the *Republic,* Plato begins resolving this tension by giving priority to individual choice. In Book IX, he renews his claim that the "inner man" (*entos anthropos*) has "absolute mastery" (*egkratestatos*) over the person (*Rep.* 589B). The two major tasks of the ruling guardians now become clear. First, they make and enforce laws for those who never become sufficiently mature to govern themselves. Second, they arrange education so youths can be brought to the point where the best part of themselves (the rational part of their soul) will take over and become their ruling guardian—"and then we set it free" (*kai tote de eleutheron aphiemen*; *Rep.* 590D–591A). Self-rule and freedom, not conformity to the directives of the ruling elite, are the goals of education in the *Republic*. Education prepares young people to become their own philosopher-rulers.

What remains unclear at the end of the *Republic* is how often education succeeds in making people wise and free. Certainly the guardian-rulers reach that stage—they rule themselves as well as the city. Can anybody else achieve the same moral maturity? It is difficult to say. The assistants to the guardians do achieve some understanding of the reason behind the laws but they never achieve personal autonomy since their lives remain ruled by the guardians. The majority of people, however, the class we are calling the workers, understand little and hence the best they can do is let the wisdom of the guardians guide them. They never become truly virtuous, they never live truly good lives because they simply do not have the education and wisdom to govern themselves. Only in freedom and self-rule is authentic humanity achieved.

However, Plato's conception of who can become truly virtuous begins to expand after he wrote the *Republic*. The famous doctrine of the Forms or Ideas plays less of a role in Plato's later ethics, and the cognitive terms *sophia* (wisdom) and *episteme* (scientific knowledge) associated with theoretical and scientific knowledge give way to the nonscientific terminology of *phronesis* (prudence) and *alethes doxa* (true opinion—something that does not even count as knowledge or wisdom in the *Republic*). Plato comes to see that the wisdom we need in ethics is not based on the Forms grasped by what the *Republic* calls *episteme*. The knowledge that we need in ethics is far more practical and context-based; it is a knowledge close to the wisdom of common sense and well-grounded opinion. In human affairs, as Aristotle will insist, we simply do not get the certitude and universality we get, or think we get, in wisdom and science.

Prudence in the *Philebus*

We can see this transformation occurring in a later dialogue, the *Philebus*, which we considered briefly in chapter 1. The dialogue is inaccurately named because it is almost entirely a discussion between Socrates and Protarchus, not Philebus. And the dialogue is usually misrepresented as a work about pleasure when the main topic is actually prudence (*phronesis*).

The dialogue begins with a discussion about what is the greatest good. Protarchus defends Philebus's view that the greatest good in life is delight, pleasure, and enjoyment. Socrates begins by arguing that the greatest good is prudence (*phronein*), thinking (*noein*), remembering, right opinions, and true reasoning. Notably absent in Socrates' argument is an emphasis on his traditional term *sophia* (wisdom). In essence, the beginning of the debate centers on whether pleasure or prudence is the key to having a good life.

Soon Socrates has Protarchus agreeing that neither option is sufficient for a good life. Rather, a good life will be a mixture of both prudence and pleasure (*Phil.* 22B, 60D–E, 61A–B). Wisdom, whether understood as *sophia* or *phronesis*, is not enough for a good life, as Socrates had originally claimed; we need pleasure as well. Wisdom, of course, was all one needed for a good life according to Socrates in the early dialogues. His position here is radically new. Plato's Socrates is now claiming, unlike the Socrates of the early dialogues, that wisdom and virtue are not sufficient for happiness and a good life because pleasure, which is neither wisdom nor a virtue, is also essential.

What becomes interesting for understanding Plato's doctrine of practical wisdom or prudence are the last sections of the dialogue where the discussion turns to just how prudence (*phronesis*) and pleasure are to be mixed. The upshot of the discussion will show how the *Philebus* provides a major influence on Aristotle and his doctrine of prudence.

Socrates begins by asking Protarchus if subjects such as arithmetic, geometry, and logical reasoning are of two kinds—those practiced by philosophers and those practiced by people actually involved in building things and conducting business. After Protarchus agrees that there are two kinds of reasoning Socrates then says that there must be two kinds of knowledge (*episteme*)—the knowledge of philosophers that grasps the eternal unchanging realities (the Forms or Ideas) and the knowledge of people engaged in the temporal changing realities of everyday life. Protarchus readily admits this and then agrees that the knowledge of the Forms is "more true" (*alethestere*) than the knowledge of transitory realities (*Phil.* 61E).

It is important to note in passing that Socrates' talk of two kinds of knowledge (*episteme*) here is quite different from what Plato had him say in the *Republic*. In the *Republic* knowledge (*episteme*) was confined to eternal unchanging realities (the mathematical objects and the Forms) and our grasp of the changing transitory realities in the world where we actually live and work was not considered knowledge but only opinion (*doxa*). In the *Philebus*, however, Plato depicts Socrates expanding the conception of knowledge (*episteme*) so that it includes not only remembrance of the Forms but apprehension of truths about the world of time, change, and history. Plato is beginning to recognize, as Aristotle will do more clearly, a place for more than mere opinion about the constantly changing realm of human life; he now admits that we can actually have knowledge about this realm as well.

Once Protarchus identifies the "more truthful" and certain knowledge—the knowledge of the eternal Forms—Socrates asks whether this "more truthful" knowledge is sufficient for living our lives. That would be ridiculous, says Protarchus. Then for living a good life we will also need, Socrates points out, feigning astonishment, knowledge that is "not firm and not genuine" but a kind of skill (*ten ou bebaion oude katharan techne*; *Phil.* 62B). While skilled workers rely on knowledge, it is not the knowledge of Forms possessed by the philosophers; rather, it is a practical and experiential knowledge.

The practical knowledge involved in making things and conducting business, of course, is the knowledge possessed by the working class in the *Republic* and in that dialogue it was not considered true knowledge or of any value in ethics. Yet in the *Philebus* Socrates leads Protarchus to say that this practical knowledge "is necessary if any one of us is going to find the way home consistently" (*Phil.* 62C). Then Socrates asks: "Shall I open the door and let all kinds of knowledge (*pasas tas epistemas*) in and let the inferior (experiential) knowledge mix with the genuine (philosophical) knowledge?" Protarchus sees no harm in doing this so

Socrates acknowledges a place for nonphilosophical practical knowledge in living our lives (*Phil.* 62D–E). It is not enough to know the unchanging transcendent Ideas, not enough to know the definitions of justice, temperance, and courage that were so important in the *Republic.* We also need to know how to find our way around the world in which we live. We need knowledge of things that are temporal and changing, and this knowledge, while not as true and permanent as the knowledge of transcendent realities, is crucial for figuring out how to live.

The good life will be a mixture of pleasure and prudence, and the imperfect knowledge that comes with practical wisdom is important along with the perfect knowledge of the philosophers that comes with knowledge of the unchanging eternal Forms. Plato is not rejecting his earlier idea that to rule ourselves we need philosophical knowledge of the Forms—the definitions of the virtues— but in the *Philebus* he extends the "knowledge" we need so that it includes a far more tentative component. He now recognizes a kind of practical knowledge that is true knowledge despite being less certain than what was considered knowledge in the *Republic.*

This practical knowledge is very close to what the workers do when they make things. It is a skill, a *techne* (*Rep.* 59E). When we mix pleasure and prudence to make a good life, we are not acting like philosophers contemplating the Forms but like the artisans who make things. And people making things often rely on true opinion, which was not really knowledge at all according to the *Republic* because it is about transitory things and not the eternal and unchanging Forms (*Rep.* 59A).

The emphasis on the practical side of *phronesis* in the *Philebus* represents a broadening of Plato's views from those in Book IV of the *Republic* where Socrates contrasted the knowledge of the philosopher-rulers with the practical knowledge of craftsmen, and said that only the former—knowledge of the Forms—is rightly called wisdom or *sophia* (*Rep.* 428B–429A). And in Book VI of the *Republic,* Socrates, discussing what constitutes the good, spoke somewhat disparagingly of those who say it is prudence (*phronesis*). In the *Philebus,* however, the term most often used to designate the key cognitive virtue for living a good life is *phronesis.*

Prudence in the *Statesman*

A brief look at later works of Plato confirms that the mature Plato came to feel that many more people than the elite guardians of the *Republic* could achieve the prudence necessary for authentic virtue. The *Statesman*, as the title indicates, is about political rulers but it is also concerned with the kinds of people needed to make a state function well. Of particular importance for the state, Plato tells us, are people with military expertise (generals) as well as judges, orators, and educators. It is the section on educators that catches our attention. The educators' job is to impart the knowledge necessary to bring a great number of citizens to a life of virtue; that is, a life of self-rule. Underlying the educators' role is the idea that a successful state needs a good number of virtuous citizens.

The education Plato has in mind is the education that will culminate in authentic virtue, and the character presenting his views in the *Statesman* is identified simply as the "stranger." The stranger first acknowledges that not everyone can be educated to virtue. Some people are by nature evil and have no capacity for virtues such as courage and temperance—these, the ruler will have to punish or exile. Others are simply too ignorant and abject—these, the ruler will make slaves. But the rest of the people can, with education, become wise enough for authentic virtue (*St.* 308E–309A).

The stranger then points out that most people naturally fall into two main psychological types. One group has a natural tendency toward anger; they fight for what they see as right and do not hesitate to be confrontational. The other group has a natural tendency toward moderation and compromise; they seek harmony instead of confrontation. In other words, some people tend by nature toward the virtue of courage, others toward the virtue of temperance.

The educator's task is to take these two groups, each with its dominant virtuous tendency, and bring them to authentic virtue by weaving into their lives the virtue they are missing. And how does the educator do this? According to Socrates in the *Meno* and Plato himself in the *Republic*, only wisdom and knowledge will make a person authentically virtuous. But the *Statesman* gives a different answer: authentic moral virtue can now be achieved "by reliable true *opinion* (*alethe doxan meta bebaiseos*) about things that are noble (*kalon*), just, and good"(*St.* 309C). The wisdom and knowledge that Plato championed in the *Republic* are apparently still the ideal, but few can achieve it. The rest of us will have to make ethical decisions without the philosopher's *sophia* (wisdom) and *episteme* (knowledge); we have to rely on *phonesis* (prudence) and *doxa* (opinion), but these are enough because opinions about what is noble, just, and good can be, with education, reliable and true.

Reliable true opinions are not guesses but reasonable opinions; that is, the person holding them can give reasons for what he holds. In the earlier *Meno* Socrates acknowledged that opinions could be true but he insisted that they would always be unreliable because the person would not be able to give any good reasons for them. In the *Statesman*, however, Plato is now saying that good reasons can be given for some opinions and that these opinions are reliable.

Reliable and true opinions are inferior to the truth that philosophical knowledge (*episteme*) gives us but they are enough for people to make good ethical decisions. In the *Statesman*, a person no longer needs knowledge (*episteme*) to determine what is good. Now a reasonable, well-formed opinion (*doxa*) is enough. Ethics has lost the rigor it had when it was confined to theoretical knowledge and wisdom, yet it has gained a much wider potential audience by acknowledging the value of practical knowledge, prudence, and reliable true opinion.

The educators in the *Statesman* are important because they help people see reasons for being temperate, courageous, and just, and thereby choose these virtues for themselves. The educators do not rule people; they help people acquire prudence so they can rule their own lives well. In the *Republic* the best most people could do was to follow those who had achieved theoretical wisdom—the philosopher-rulers. Now, in the *Statesman*, the educators help many citizens acquire enough practical wisdom or prudence to follow the rational part of their own souls. Most of us will never achieve the knowledge of the philosopher-rulers but we can achieve reliable reasonable opinion, which is enough for making the choices that create authentic virtue.

Prudence in the *Laws*

Plato's insistence that the state needs virtuous citizens and that virtue rests on people achieving the prudence to direct their own lives appears again in what was probably his last work, the *Laws*. As were the *Republic* and the *Statesman*, the *Laws* is about political theory, about how best to run a city-state. And as in the *Statesman*, Plato distances himself from the *Republic* in several ways. He has lost confidence in government by the guardian-rulers that he recommended in the *Republic*; he no longer thinks it can work. The knowledge a ruling guardian needs is too difficult to obtain and even if someone were to obtain it once in power he would almost inevitably become corrupted by selfish actions (*Laws* 875A–C). Hence, what we need is not an elite group of guardian rulers but a set of laws to govern the city. Government must be of laws, not of men and women as it was in the *Republic*.

The laws that Plato envisions in the *Laws* for his imaginary new city of Magnesia in southern Crete will be extraordinarily comprehensive and detailed, and some intrude deeply into what we consider private life. Marriage, for example, will be heavily regulated by a committee of women, which will supervise marriages for the first ten years; should no children arrive within ten years, the couple will be expected to divorce. Various penalties, including imprisonment and death, will be given to those guilty of heresy or atheism (*Laws* 899D–905D). Homosexuality will be outlawed (*Laws* 836C–E) and other sexual activity regulated (*Laws* 838D–842A). Foreign travel will also be restricted (*Laws* 950D–951C). Such laws, along with all other laws, are for the common good, and the citizen is expected to follow them. In keeping with the recognition that people need to know the reasons for what they do, the laws will have preambles that present the rationale behind each law.

Of interest to our project, however, is not the political theory in the book; rather, it is the assumptions about virtue ethics that underlie it. In the very first book of this long treatise, the Athenian stranger, who is the chief spokesman, points out that laws function rightly when they bring about the happiness (*eudaimonia*) of those who follow them by providing the goods they need to live well. These goods are of two kinds, ordinary human goods and extraordinary or "divine" (*theia*) goods. Ordinary human goods include health, attractiveness, strength, and wealth. The extraordinary goods are prudence, temperance, courage, and justice. And of these prudence is the primary virtue. The human goods are subordinate to the "divine" goods, and the divine goods in turn are subordinate to prudence (*Laws* 631B–D).

The language could hardly be more explicit. The ultimate goal of the laws is *the happiness of the citizens*. This happiness consists of good things in life: ordinary human goods such as health and the extraordinary goods, which are the virtues. And the chief virtue is prudence. Laws are not the last word; they are good only if they contribute to people's happiness by enhancing good things in their lives, especially their prudence. Only those people capable of ruling themselves (*archein auton*) are good; those incapable of ruling themselves are bad (*Laws* 644B). However, it is difficult to say how many people can actually achieve the knowledge and maturity that Plato says are required for self-governance. Plato's remarks often leave us with an impression that is widespread in the ancient world—virtue is demanding and most people never really achieve it; that is, most people never manage to live truly good and happy lives. Hence, laws will be needed because most people will not or cannot direct their own lives well.

However, the Athenian stranger leaves no doubt about the priority of the individual over the state. He reminds his two partners in the dialogue that no individual should let any obstacle stand in the way of achieving the primary goal of living a good and virtuous life, not even his country or state. If the laws of the state hinder rather than help a person achieve happiness then the person can try to change the laws. If this does not work, he will abide by the helpful laws but reject the unhelpful ones, or he will revolt, or he will leave to live in another state (*Laws* 770D–771A). The bottom line is human flourishing—*eudaimonia*, living a good and flourishing life. The laws of a good state help us do that. But not every state is good, and not all laws of good states are good, so prudence may direct a person to reject laws, or to rise up in revolt, or to go into exile and seek refuge in another state where he can achieve happiness.

No state, no law, no political authority can be recognized unless it contributes to the person's happiness. Good laws provide a tremendous support system for living a good and happy life, and thus allegiance to them is a great benefit. The laws calling for education, for heath care, for settling disputes, for restraining criminal activity, for providing law enforcement and public safety, for securing defense against enemies, and so forth, are of immense value in making any community a good place to live. But the whole purpose of the state and its laws is to help people become virtuous, and the way individuals become truly virtuous is by developing the virtue of prudence and ruling their own lives.

Plato leaves us with an interesting picture. The indispensable condition for living well and achieving happiness is a well-ruled city-state. A good state requires good laws, and the legislators need both the knowledge of philosophy (*episteme*) and skillful practical knowledge (*techne*), especially the latter, to make good laws. The aim of laws is helping people achieve happiness. Happiness is constituted of good things in life, and the indispensable good things needed for happiness or living well are the character virtues. To acquire character virtues people must achieve by education and experience the maturity to rule themselves by making their own choices in life thanks to the key virtue, prudence. The laws thus exist only to produce people who will not need the laws for ethical decision making as soon as they are able to rule themselves with prudence.

Laws are a pre-ethical stage. While they orient a person to virtue, acting because the law obliges one to act is not truly virtuous. One does not achieve a good and flourishing human life by following laws. Virtue only begins when the personal deliberation and choice characteristic of prudence orients our natural good tendencies toward what is truly good for us; that is, toward what will bring us happiness as we live.

Plato's virtue ethics is far from theories of morality that rely on moral laws, principles, and rules to determine what a person's obligations are in particular situations. Plato insists on laws and rules but following them is not what constitutes authentic virtue ethics. Authentic ethics requires the self-governance of prudence. In Plato's schema, the modern theories of laws, principles, and rules would be examples of a pre-ethical stage in our development that we will transcend once we are able to rely on prudence to make decisions and to develop the truly moral virtues in our lives.

CHAPTER 5

Prudence in Aristotle

Prudence in the *Rhetoric*

The seminal texts for understanding Aristotle's virtue of prudence are the *Nicomachean Ethics*, the *Eudemian Ethics*, and the *Politics*. However, an earlier work, the *Rhetoric*, contains helpful hints about the centrality of prudence for virtue.

Rhetoric, according to Aristotle, is not a pejorative or morally suspect term. Rhetoric is skill in constructing and delivering speeches that will guide an audience to accept what is true and good. These speeches fall into three major genres: political speeches, where people deliberate and debate about what to do; praise-giving speeches, where people extol the praiseworthy deeds of others; and legal speeches, where people prosecute and defend cases before juries acting as judges.

In all three settings, the speech needs to present sound arguments supporting the speaker's position. A successful speech, however, needs more than sound arguments. It must also arouse appropriate emotions in the audience and it must reveal that the speaker is a person of good character—a virtuous person.

Rhetoric is thus not far from ethics for several reasons. First, if one of the things that makes a speech credible is the virtuous character of the speaker then rhetoric will say something about virtue and about the role of prudence in developing virtuous character.

Second, speeches given during political debates require the speaker to know something about what makes lives good because the goal of politics, according to Aristotle, is helping people achieve good lives. And the good is defined in the *Rhetoric* in terms of prudence—it is "a practical good; it is what all living things would choose if they had prudence" (*Rh.* I, 7, 21).

Third, speeches praising great people and great deeds require the speaker to know something about virtue because virtue is the greatest of all admirable things. The *Rhetoric* defines virtue as "the capacity for acquiring and preserving good things, and the capacity for disposing one to do good in many and great ways; in fact, in all ways in all things" (*Rh.* I, 9, 4). It lists individual virtues such as justice, courage, temperance, wisdom (*sophia*), prudence, generosity, dignity, and so forth, as well as individual vices such as injustice, cowardice, intemperance, and stinginess, and then concludes by saying that "prudence is the virtue of intelligence that enables people to deliberate well about these good and bad things in regard to happiness" (*Rh.* I, 9, 5–13).

Although the *Rhetoric* gives us some important clues to Aristotle's views on prudence and its role in creating virtue and a good life, the major text for understanding this virtue is the *Nicomachean Ethics*. This work has been the subject of immense commentary and varied interpretations for centuries. Despite the controversies, the main points of the text seem clear as Aristotle expands the notion of *phronesis* we find in Plato's later works.

Prudence and Authentic Character Virtue

As already noted in chapter 3, Aristotle follows Plato in distinguishing two major "parts" of the soul—the rational part and the nonrational part. Each part has its own set of virtues: intellectual virtues belong to the rational part and character virtues belong to the nonrational part. Plato and Aristotle agree that both the character virtues and the intellectual virtues are indispensable components of living a good life, a life of happiness. Aristotle, however, has a much more developed account than Plato on how these virtues develop and interact.

Aristotle reminds us that the character virtues develop as the result of repeated actions. Just as we become builders by building things repeatedly and harpists by playing the harp repeatedly, we become just and temperate by performing just and temperate actions repeatedly (NE 1103a33–b2). And we become wise and skilled and prudent by being wise and skilled and prudent repeatedly. However, simply repeating the appropriate actions is not enough to develop *authentic* character virtues in our lives. Aristotle, as we have seen, insists that actions arising from natural tendencies or in response to external factors develop only natural virtue (*phusike arete*) and not authentic virtue (*kuria arete*). This means that they do not lead to happiness and the good life that we ultimately seek in ethics. This is so because natural virtues do not involve the most important part of the soul, the rational part that Aristotle considers the hallmark of our humanity (NE 1144b1–17). Without deliberation and the personal decision to perform the action for its own sake—that is, because it is truly good—there is no authentic character virtue. An agent develops character virtues "only if he is in a certain (psychological) state as he acts; that is, he knows what he is doing, makes a decision to do it, and is firm and unshaken as he does it" (NE 1105a29–34).

Prudence is thus the origin of the authentic character virtues. Those possessing it deliberate, decide, and direct themselves toward the ultimate goal of life—happiness. Unless people mature to the point where they knowingly and deliberately choose to perform virtuous actions for their own sake, they never become truly virtuous. Simply put, performing truly virtuous action, forming a truly virtuous character, or becoming a truly virtuous person hinges on whether or not the person acquires the knowledge and maturity to deliberate and make good decisions, and then carry them out precisely because the actions decided upon are seen as good. Only those people managing and directing their own lives in accord with what they see are truly virtuous. According to Aristotle, "[t]he virtues are decisions of some kind or (at least) do not occur without decision-making" (NE 1106a4–5).

Prudence and Autonomy

An essential condition for making prudential decisions and choosing virtuous actions for their own sake is that the decision maker possesses a significant degree of autonomy. Actions that develop authentic virtue must be voluntary (NE 1109b32–35). By "voluntary," Aristotle means that the virtuous action must be chosen freely; it cannot occur without knowledge or be forced. By "forced," he means *physically* forced, as when a person is pushed, tortured, drugged, or otherwise similarly coerced. Threats, even of grave harm that will follow if we do not do something, diminish our autonomy but really do not destroy it according to Aristotle. Faced with threats, we have to weigh the goods and "bads" involved and choose the less worse option, recognizing that some things are so heinous that the virtuous person cannot deliberately choose to do them no matter how terrible the threats.

Aristotle's insistence on free choice and responsibility runs deep. The virtuous person never says "I had no choice" when simply facing threats. The bank teller looking at the barrel of a gun may hand over the money to the robber, but the teller does not do this because there was "no choice." Rather, he or she does it because he or she decided that it was the *prudent* thing to do in the situation. Aristotle gives an example from a lost play of Euripedes, the *Alcmaeon*, that shows how much he thinks we are responsible for what we do. The father of Alcmaeon ordered him, under threat of dire consequences, to kill his mother. Alcmaeon apparently did so and then defended himself by saying he was compelled to obey his father and thus had no choice. Aristotle does not agree. He insists that action under threat is still voluntary; therefore, Alcmaeon should not have killed his mother in these circumstances despite the terrible consequences that would befall him for disobeying his powerful father (NE 1110a26–29).

Prudence and Prudent People (the *phronimoi*)

To help us learn what prudence is and how it works, Aristotle makes what first appears to be an extraordinary move. He tells us that we learn about prudence not by studying moral theory (or by reading books such as this one!) but by looking at or studying people living virtuous and good lives (NE 1140a25). We understand what *phronesis* is and how it works by watching the *phronimoi*, the people who have it and manage their lives well. We learn how to be prudent by watching how prudent people live their lives. Prudent people are the virtuous people; we learn about virtue by watching how they live virtuously. We learn how to live a successful human life by looking at those who are already doing it.

Ironically, the word Aristotle uses here for "looking at" (watching, studying) prudent people practicing the virtue of prudence is *theoreo*, the root of the word "theory" in English. Theorizing in Aristotle's ethics is not about developing moral theories but about looking at people living truly good lives. We watch how they successfully manage their lives, and, from their example, we learn how to manage successfully our own lives. We learn about *phronesis* by watching how the *phronimoi* practice it.

Watching how truly virtuous people live enables us to see five major features of prudence. First, prudence is a deliberately acquired permanent state; second, prudence makes effective decisions; third, prudence is a truth-attaining reasoning; forth, prudence relies on experience; and fifth, prudence is the norm for moral action. We will now explore each of these features.

Prudence Is a Deliberately Acquired State

Truly prudent people are prudent day in and day out. Prudence exists in their lives as a permanent state. As we noted in chapter 3, the word "state" rather than "habit" seems the appropriate translation for Aristotle's word *hexis*. Sometimes *hexis* is translated as "habit," which the dictionaries certainly allow. Unfortunately, however, this translation masks an important point. What Aristotle means by *hexis* is not quite the same thing as a habit, which is normally designated by the Greek word *ethos* (spelled with *eta*, the short "e"). Both states and habits are acquired by repeated actions, but for Aristotle, they differ in this respect: states develop from repeated actions that are thoughtful and deliberate; habits develop from repeated actions that are not thoughtful and deliberate.

The distinction between a habit (*ethos* with the short "e") and a state (*hexis*) is important in Aristotle because it coincides with his distinction between natural and authentic virtue. The natural virtues are indeed correctly described as habits because they are acquired without being chosen for their own sakes. The authentic virtues, on the other hand, can only be acquired by being deliberately chosen for their own sakes. Hence, they are more than habits; they are deliberately acquired states. Prudence is a state of mind acquired thoughtfully and deliberately for its own sake.

Prudence Makes Effective Decisions

Prudence is *the* decision-making virtue. The virtue of prudence not only designates a deliberately acquired state but an activity—the activity of making decisions that lead to concrete actions. In fact, it is the deliberately chosen prudent actions that produce the state of prudence. As with any authentic virtue, the actions produce the state (*hexis*); we become prudent by making prudent decisions repeatedly.

Aristotle distinguishes three major phases in the exercise of prudence: deliberation (*bouleusis*), the decision itself (*prohairesis*), and the command (*epitaktike*) that leads to action. We need to say a few words about each phase.

Deliberation is figuring out what particular action in a particular situation will likely contribute to our doing well and living well. Deliberation is figuring out what move in a particular situation will likely achieve the overriding good of a human life—happiness. The hallmark of prudence is deliberation: "For we say that deliberating well (*eu boueuesthai*) is most especially the proper work (*ergon*) of the prudent person." (NE 1141b10–11)

Aristotle reminds us that deliberation is not about things that are fixed. We do not deliberate about the sum of two plus two or about the laws of physics. What we deliberate about is what we can choose to do or not to do. Our choices are not fixed, thus we need to deliberate to see whether it is good for us to do or not do something. Our fundamental desire is the rational desire (*boulesis*) for a good life, yet we never know for sure in many cases just what move in particular situations will help us achieve this goal. So we have to deliberate about what to do and, if there are several good courses of action, about which one is most likely to help us reach our goal in the best way. Furthermore, if the issue is a major one in our lives, we should then seek the advice of others in our deliberation (NE 1112b9–20).

Deliberation leads to the second phase of prudence—making a decision. Aristotle distinguishes decision making (*prohairesis*) from simple choice (*hairesis*). Decisions follow rational deliberation about what to do in view of an end while choices do not. If a person simply elects to do something without deliberating then it is a choice, not a decision, because decision is always preceded by deliberation. Aristotle felt that children and even animals make choices but not decisions. A child can choose to climb out of the crib and a cat can choose a quiet place to nap, but the child and the cat do not truly engage in decision making because they do not deliberate rationally about how climbing out of a crib or taking a quiet nap will achieve an end. Decision making in virtue ethics involves deliberating about what we think will bring us happiness.

Making a decision, however, is not enough for virtue. If prudence went no further than deliberating and deciding what would be good for a person to do or avoid it would fail as a practical virtue because the action decided upon might never be done. Decisions must lead to action if the person is to become truly virtuous and actually live a good life. This brings us to the third phase of prudence—it commands that the action decided upon actually be done (NE 1143a9). Prudence does more than deliberate and decide—it commands the person to perform the action decided upon. Prudence deliberates, decides, and then orders and executes the decision.

There is a difference, then, between making prudential decisions and making moral judgments. Judgments are not decisions because they do not require personal action. People can make judgments about the morality of abortion or of capital punishment, for example, but many of them will never have to make a decision about having or performing an abortion, or about condemning a person to death. Prudence occurs only when the person deliberating is actually deciding about something that she or he will actually do. Unlike a judgment, decisions made by prudence always command the deliberating person to do or not to do something. Prudence is about something that I personally face: "Prudence is prescriptive for its goal is determining what one must do or not do" (NE 1143a8–10).

Virtue ethics is thus autonomous and prescriptive; the agent's prudential reasoning identifies what is good and then commands him or her to act. Prudence is a profoundly practical intellectual virtue because it actually moves the person to act in one way rather than another. It is not merely the intellectual exercise of making a judgment; it actually moves the doer to do something. Prudence is the cause or source (the *arche*, the principle) of deliberate human action.

Prudence is an intellectual virtue and yet moves the agent to act. How can this be? How can thought give rise to action? Philosophers have argued about this for centuries. Many claim that reason alone can never move us to action; only feelings or appetites can do this. Aristotle himself admits that "thought (*dianoia*) by itself moves nothing" (NE 1138a35). So how can prudence, a virtue of thought—a *dianoetike arete*—move us?

Aristotle's answer is subtle. Prudence is a matter of thought, thus an intellectual virtue, but it is more than thought—it is also desire. Aristotle is careful to show that desire is a part of prudence. Desire is what motivates us to deliberate, to decide, and then to do what decision directs. Unlike Plato, who located all desires in the nonrational part of the soul, Aristotle identifies a desire in the rational part of the soul itself, a desire he calls *boulesis*. A rational desire is other than the desires of the appetites and feelings that reside in the nonrational part of the soul. *Boulesis* is the rational desire for what is truly good in action (the appetites desire pleasure and the feelings desire only what appears good). Rational desire requires knowledge to grasp what is truly good in action and knowledge of what is good in action requires rational desire if the agent is actually to perform the good action.

Thus Aristotle famously says that we can describe effective decision making as either "desirous understanding" (*orektikos nous*) or "thoughtful desire" (*orexis dianoetike*; NE 1139b4–5). We could loosely translate the phrases as "desirous mind" and "mindful desire." His point is that prudence can be equally well described as thought embracing a rational desire or as a rational desire embracing thought. These equivalent phrases show how prudential decision making involves both knowledge and desire. Without deliberation, we would never know and decide what is truly good; without desire, we would never do what we know is truly good. And, of course, in virtue ethics, deliberately doing what is good is the only thing that develops the authentic character virtues and makes a human life good.

Prudence Is a Truth-Attaining Reasoning

The third major feature of prudence that we notice from watching the people who practice it is this: they rely on reasoning as they figure out what is good or bad for their lives. Aristotle defines prudence as "a state achieving truth by means of reason (*meta logou*) about what is good or bad for a human being concerning action" (NE 1140b6–7, see also 1140b20–21).

The kind of reasoning Aristotle has in mind for deliberation is important. It is neither the demonstrative syllogistic reasoning of science (*episteme*) that is based on necessary immutable principles, nor the practical reasoning of the crafts (*techne*) that can be summarized and taught as a systematically organized body of instructions. The reasoning involved in prudence is primarily a flexible on-the-spot reasoning that assesses the situation and looks for a good move.

Prudential reasoning, which is not the reasoning we use in science or in practicing skills, and which is not simply guessing, is figuring out how to behave in the situation we face in order to achieve something truly good for ourselves. Thus, a thief who figures out how to rob a bank is not reasoning well because he is not figuring out how to achieve something truly good. The thief might be quite clever, but cleverness is never confused with the reasoning called prudence. Prudential reasoning is always oriented toward a good, and something is truly good when it contributes to the ultimate good of living—happiness.

Good prudential reasoning, mindful of the ultimate good, rationally figures out the right thing to do in the right way at the right time (NE 1142b28). The right thing to do in the right way at the right time, of course, is whatever brings the person closer to the ultimate good in life—living well, happiness. Or, in Aristotle's words:

"Quite simply, a good deliberator is competent at figuring out through reasoning what is the best good for a human being in actions" (NE 1141b12). To figure this out in each particular situation, the prudent person needs to know general truths about what is good for human beings. The agent needs to know that it is usually good to be temperate, courageous, just, loving, and so forth. And one needs to know that other things are good for human beings—health, money, friends, supportive political systems, and so forth. More important, however, the prudent person needs to perceive the particular elements in the situation. Here, experience is important, and the person with experience of particulars often makes better decisions than the person with general knowledge. Aristotle offers a cryptic example: when it comes to eating well, the general knowledge that light meats are easily digested is not absolutely necessary; all the person needs to know is the particular truth that he digests chicken well, which is drawn from the trial and error of experience (NE 1141b14–24).

Prudence Relies on Experience

This brings us to the fourth major feature of prudence—its reliance on experience. Experience is crucial in moral decision making. Prudence is above all concerned with particulars—a particular person in a particular situation is making a particular decision about a particular action in an effort to achieve a particular life that will be good and bring personal happiness—and understanding particulars comes only from experience. Young people lack the experience needed for prudent decision making even though they can do well at understanding science and mathematics (NE 1142a12–21). The insights and beliefs of experienced older people are important when it comes to making decisions in particular situations because "experience has given these people an eye to see correctly" (NE 1143b14).

Prudence is based on the personal experience of actually living a moral life. Its truth is practical because it is based on human experience, not on theories about how we ought to live. The theoretical knowledge found in moral theories is not capable of resolving the problems that people encounter in trying to live well. Only the knowledge rooted in virtuous character and gained by experience offers reliable guidance. The virtuous person, not the moral philosopher, is the better guide for ethical action.

Aristotle is not the only ancient ethicist to stress experience and prudence over moral philosophy. Epicurus' *Letter to Menoeceus* echoes the same thought.

> The source of all these things (that enable us to achieve happiness) and the best good is prudence (*phronesis*). Hence prudence is more valuable than philosophy (*philosophia*), and from it all the remaining virtues come into being. (Long and Sedley, *The Hellenistic Philosophers* 2:21B)

Aristotle's position regarding the need for personal experience in ethics is radical. In order to say something worthwhile about ethics and virtue, a person must first be ethical and virtuous; otherwise, the conclusions will be unreliable. Unfortunately, "most people (*hoi polloi*) do not perform virtuous actions; they take refuge in reasoning [about them] and they imagine that they are doing philosophy and becoming good in this way" (NE 1105b12–15). Reasoning about and discussing ethical issues does not make us good; we become good only by deliberately performing virtuous actions.

Prudence Is the Norm for Moral Action

The moral norm that virtuous people, the *phronimoi*, live by is their own prudential reasoning. Their ethical criterion is not whether what they do is in accord with any moral laws, principles, or rules; it is whether what they do is in accord with right reason (*kata ton orthon logon*), a phrase that appears repeatedly in the *Nicomachean Ethics* (NE 1103b31; 1107a1; 1115b12, 19; 1117a8; 1119a20, b18; 1125b35; 1138a10, b20–34; 1144b23–28; 1147b3, 31; 1151a12, 22). It also occurs in the *Eudemian Ethics* (EE 1220b19; 1222a8, b5). There is no doubt that the frequently used phrase "according to right reason" refers to prudence: "The right reasoning about this matter (virtue) is prudence." (*orthos de logos peri ton toiouton e phronesis estin*; NE 1144b27).

Aristotle hastens to add that "in accord with right reason" has to be understood in an active sense. It is not enough that the person's action happens to be in accord with right reason or prudence; the agent's prudential reasoning must actually decide that the action is virtuous. Virtue is more than action "in accord with" (*kata*) right reason; it is action arrived at "by means of" (*meta*) right reason (NE 1144b26–27). For an action to be virtuous or moral the person must engage personally in the prudential reasoning that leads to the decision.

Aristotle thus concludes that Socrates was only partly right when he said that virtue is knowledge. He was wrong to reduce all the virtues to knowledge but right to say that "virtue cannot exist without (the knowledge gained from) prudence" (NE 1144b18–21). There is no doubt as to Aristotle's point. The virtue of prudence creates the character virtues: "For once the one virtue of prudence is present, all the virtues are present" (NE 1145a1).

The great fear of many is that leaving ethics to what prudent people decide for themselves will result in a deplorable subjectivity. What is needed, they argue, is something transcendent or transcendental, some universal unchanging norm that will provide moral laws, principles, maxims, rules, or rights to serve as the ultimate criterion of moral decision making. Unless there is something like a transcendent universal moral law either coming from God (divine law) or embedded in nature (natural law), or universal rights possessed by all human beings, or the Kantian transcendental categorical imperative with its demand for universal application, or the universal utilitarian principle of the greatest happiness for the greatest number, their fear is that ethics will degenerate into subjectivism and relativism where everyone simply decides what is right or wrong for themselves.

This may have been the great fear of some medieval theologians and explain to some extent why Thomas Aquinas saw the need to graft Ulpian's natural law doctrine onto Aristotle's ethics and to integrate both virtue and natural law with divine law. And it may have been the great fear of Kant, who insisted that prudence would never do because ethical maxims need a transcendental foundation no less than do the universal laws of scientific reasoning (the "synthetic *a priori* judgments" of the *Critique of Pure Reason*), which he found in Newtonian science, in geometry, and in mathematics.

Aristotle's notion of prudential prescriptive decision making can easily be distorted to make it look like crass relativism. As "Joe College" might say on first hearing of Aristotle's ethics: "This virtue ethics is great; the goal of life is happiness and the virtue of prudence means I get to decide what makes me happy." But the accusation of relativism is not a worthy objection to Aristotle's account because it betrays a gross misunderstanding of what he means. Aristotle never locates the criterion of ethical decision making in what I think will make me happy and what I think will make my life good. He locates it in the practical reasoning that discerns, to the extent it can be discerned, what will truly create happiness and what will truly make my life good. The criterion so understood implies an objective dimension: the goal of prudence is to discern what will *in fact* make my life good.

The worry that adopting a virtue ethics rooted in prudence will make ethics totally subjective and relative is largely exaggerated and, if virtue ethics is correctly understood, impossible. Authentic prudence is a *virtue,* and something is a virtue only if it really makes a life good. The good life sought in prudence, as we saw, is not what appears to be good or what I think is good; it is what is actually a good human life. Prudence is about truth, practical truth to be sure, but truth nonetheless. What I happen to think does not change the fact that some things are good for me and some things are not. Prudence, correctly understood, never reduces ethics to the apparent good, to what I think is good; prudence seeks always what is truly good. It is not enough for one to think it is good to perform certain actions and therefore claim it is right to do so. Prudence means that she or he can show that the intended action is actually reasonable and that performing it will truly be a good way for a human being to live.

A more telling criticism is that Aristotle's "prudence" allowed him to tolerate such obvious immoralities as slavery and discrimination against women. But we do not judge the value and importance of virtue ethics, or of any moral theory for that matter, by pointing out lapses of judgment and cultural prejudices. Some medieval moralists, Thomas Aquinas among them, concluded by relying on a notion of natural law that masturbation was morally worse than rape and incest. And Kant, relying on maxims derived from his categorical imperative, thought that masturbation was morally worse than suicide and that telling a lie to save an innocent victim from a man bent on murdering her would always be absolutely and categorically immoral. Moreover, a prudence-based ethics focused on achieving the good in historical situations is more readily a self-correcting ethic than principle-based ethics. As soon as free men see that their societies will be more conducive to virtue if slavery and discrimination against women are eliminated, prudence directs them to move in that direction. Modifying or changing moral principles and rules tends to be a more cumbersome process.

Another telling criticism is that Aristotle's "prudence" neglects our responsibilities toward others. Prudence seems to be self-centered, to be an egoism instead of the altruism we expect from the best of ethics. But Aristotle did not think in terms of modern dichotomies such as egoism versus altruism, or liberal rights versus communitarian responsibilities, or individual good versus the common good. Prudence seeks a truly good life, and a good human life is interpersonal and political as well as personal. To say a moral agent seeks one's own good is to say that the agent seeks the good of others and of his or her communities because the personal good is inextricably entwined with the good of family, friends, and communities.

Still another criticism is that Aristotle's ethics is elitist. He does not think that most people (the *hoi polloi*) would achieve the prudence needed to manage their lives and live virtuously. Aristotle was a realist about how demanding the virtue of prudence is and he never indicates that most people are capable of managing their own lives prudently. He notes that the young are not yet capable of practicing prudence because they lack maturity and experience, and are ruled by feeling more than intelligence. But many adults also fail to achieve prudence and authentic virtue. Some adults have not been well brought up and lack a residue of natural virtue, others have chosen immoral acts for so long their characters might be permanently set, and still others are simply too vicious by nature to be virtuous. Finally, Aristotle feels that it would be practically impossible for people in positions of social subservience to have the freedom to manage their lives by making prudential decisions on their own. Hence Aristotle considers it practically impossible for slaves and women to practice prudence, a consideration he would presumably not make for societies where there are no slaves and where woman enjoy more freedom and autonomy than they did in ancient Greece.

The fact that many people cannot manage their lives with prudence because they lack virtuous natural tendencies, or did not receive moral education, or have developed bad habits, or are simply pathologically immoral, or do not have ample freedom to make decisions, or are simply unwilling to assume the responsibility does not change the fact that authentic virtue—what Aristotle called *ethics*—can only be achieved by prudence. In other words, Aristotle agrees with Plato that not everyone is able to be virtuous and live a good life because not everyone can or will practice prudence.

Admittedly this is a form of elitism; however, it is not necessarily an objectionable elitism. Not everyone has the opportunity to succeed as a carpenter, or as a nurse, or as a programmer, or as a teacher, or as a mechanic, or as a pilot, and so forth; therefore, it is not unreasonable to assume that not everyone has the opportunity to succeed at life. Moreover, Aristotle's failure to include slaves and women among those who can deliberate prudently is culturally contingent and largely irrelevant in cultures without slaves and supportive of education and opportunities for women. In other words, with education and cultural support, so many more people than those alive in Aristotle's time can join the "elite" group managing their own lives with prudence that the term loses much of its pejorative connotation.

Yet there remains a cohort of people unable or unwilling to manage their own lives well. What can they do? How should they behave? This brings us to a consideration of the next best thing to authentic virtue ethics—laws and rules.

Prudence and Laws

Although Aristotle's virtuous person has no need of moral laws, principles, or rules to guide her action because she lives by the dictates of her prudential reasoning, laws and other rule-like principles do play two important roles in Aristotle's ethics. First, good laws produce the social environment that people need for authentic virtue by curbing injustice, violence, and social upheavals.

Second, good laws channel people into good patterns of behavior that form the *natural* virtues in their lives. The laws prepare people for *authentic* virtue by exerting pressure on them to perform good actions and avoid bad actions, and thus the laws shape their character by encouraging the natural virtues (the *aretai phusikai*) that set the stage for prudence and the authentic virtues (the *aretai kuriae*). The legislative, regulative, and judicial systems of a society are thus closely allied with the natural character virtues in ethics.

However, as we noted earlier, people do not become truly virtuous by doing or not doing something because it is prescribed or proscribed by law (NE 1143b15–18). One becomes virtuous only by personally deliberating to decide to do or not do something and then doing it for its own sake because it is good. A person does not achieve authentic virtue by following laws but by following the dictates of his own prudential reasoning. Good laws—laws formulated by legislators reasoning prudently—guide people toward authentic virtue by commanding virtuous actions and forbidding nonvirtuous actions. This legal orientation is important because people need to develop by repeated actions a level of natural virtue before they can rely on their prudence to manage their own lives successfully. The ability to manage one's own life can only grow out of a character already shaped by the experience of performing good actions, and the preliminary guides for determining what actions are good are good laws, regulations, rules, court decisions, and so forth.

Prudence is not only necessary for personal decision making; legislators also need prudence. Prudence is the key virtue for making the rules and laws that will orient and protect society. Legislators, according to Aristotle, rely on prudential, not theoretical, reasoning to make and enforce the laws needed to guide the community. Political leaders need to be from the class of authentically prudent and virtuous people because they need the virtue of prudence to discern what laws will advance the human good in their society. If they have not developed prudence and achieved authentic moral virtue in their personal lives they will never be able to legislate well in their public lives. Deliberating about what laws to enact and about what regulations to promulgate is the work of prudence.

Aristotle also notes a third major area where prudence operates—the management of households. Here, too, all sorts of prudential decisions have to be made if the household is to be a nurturing environment for its members, as any parent knows all too well. In fact, whenever a person is deliberating about the human good in action and deciding to pursue it for its own sake, one is practicing prudence whether the pursuit is strictly personal, or familial, or legislative, or politically deliberative (deciding about war, education, public projects, and so forth), or judicial (Athenian courts had juries but no judges) (NE 1141b30–35).

Character Virtue without Prudence?

Toward the end of Book VI of the *Nichomachean Ethics*, which is about personal prudence, Aristotle raises an interesting and still relevant objection to his insistence on prudence as the foundational and indispensable virtue for ethics. After all, if the goal is to live a good life, and a good life is largely the work of good character giving rise to good actions, why is the personal effort of deliberation and prudence needed? What does it matter if a person follows moral laws, principles, or rules imposed by civic or religious authorities or derived from the theories of moral philosophers or theologians? If good actions are what make a life good, then it does not seem to matter what dictates a person follows. The important thing seems to be performing the good actions and living a good life, and it would seem to matter little whether the moral imperative for the action is derived from moral laws, moral authorities, or moral theories, or, as Aristotle insists, from one's own prudential reasoning.

Aristotle's reply is of interest. He says that it is crucial to rely on the dictates of personal prudence for living a truly good life, and he gives two reasons. First, living a good and fulfilling life means functioning as a complete human being and this means, above all, living as a rational being. The rational soul has two major capabilities: a theoretical capability for understanding how things are and two practical capabilities, one for making things and one for doing things. A failure to exercise the most important practical reasoning of all—the reasoning about how to do well and live well—is a failure to live life fully. It is a failure that results in an impoverished life, a life where the capability to manage one's life—prudence—remains unfulfilled. Thus personal prudential decision making is a worthwhile choice for its own sake because it fulfills an important human potential, the potential of reasoning well and choosing wisely.

Second, unless the virtuous actions are dictated by our personal decision making and done for their own sake, they do not result in *authentic* character virtue. The actions may in fact be good and thus build virtuous character; however, the result is only natural virtue (*arete physike*). Authentic or full virtue (*arete kuria*) occurs only when the person actually deliberates and personally decides to perform the virtuous actions for their own sake. Doing something because it is dictated by some kind of moral law or moral authority never results in authentic virtue, and authentic virtue is the crucial component in living a good life and achieving happiness. It does make a difference whether or not a person prudently reasons and personally decides what to do, and the difference is between being authentically virtuous and only naturally virtuous.

Authentic or full virtue depends on the personal effort to deliberate and to decide for oneself: "Authentic virtue (*arete kuria*) cannot be acquired without prudence"(NE 1144b16–17). Conceiving ethics in terms of the obligation to perform or avoid actions dictated by moral laws, principles, and rules, in Aristotle's view, misses the point. Only actions authentically chosen for their own sake after deliberation qualify for virtue ethics.

The general picture emerging from Aristotle is as follows: As Plato said, people are born with some natural tendencies toward a good life and happiness. To varying degrees they may be temperate, courageous, kind, loving, empathetic, and so forth. Education and training can improve these natural tendencies and establish what Aristotle calls "natural virtues." Once the natural virtues are established and the person has also acquired the cognitive ability to reason and deliberate prudently about his life, he can then personally choose to feel and behave in the ways that make his life go well. This is the point where authentic virtue—and authentic ethics—begins.

Aristotle is clear that there is a circular causality here. Prudence does not develop unless the person is already virtuous and a person is not virtuous until he develops prudence. In other words, a person cannot reason well about action unless he is already a good person and he cannot be a good person unless he has reasoned well about action. Put more bluntly, Aristotle defines character virtue in terms of prudence, and prudence in terms of character virtue. If the circle is not to be a vicious circle, one of its components—either character or prudence—will have to have priority. The circle is not vicious because there is a primordial priority. While it is true that prudence will not function without a *naturally* virtuous character there is no doubt that *authentic* virtuous character does not develop until and unless a person decides for herself that she will be temperate, courageous, just, and so forth.

The natural character virtues (*phusikai aretai*) bring us a long way but they are not converted to the authentic moral virtues (*kuriai aretai*) until the point where deliberation and personal decision making kick in. A person cannot make prudent choices about the appetites unless one already has some level of temperance—the natural character virtue. But character virtue at this stage only sets the stage for personal prudential reasoning. The natural character virtue of temperance converts to authentic temperance if and when personal prudential reasoning leads the agent to decide to be temperate because acting temperately is perceived as valuable for its own sake. Only at this point—when the agent begins to deliberate carefully and decide reasonably in light of what is good about the actions craved by personal appetites—does the person become authentically virtuous.

It is instructive to note that prudence, unlike the character virtues, does not have both a natural state and an authentic state. Prudence is by definition an authentic virtue. The word prudence in Aristotle never refers to natural virtue. Whenever prudence exists it is authentic virtue. Prudence can only occur as authentic virtue because it is precisely the virtue that creates all the other authentic character virtues.

CHAPTER 6

Prudence in Stoicism

Prudence and Stoic Determinism

The striking text already noted in chapter 3 reminds us how Zeno, Stoicism's founder, retained the foundational role of prudence found in Socrates, Plato, and Aristotle. Plutarch, writing around the end of the first century, reports Zeno's position as follows: "Zeno of Citium . . . defines prudence in matters of distribution as justice, (prudence) in matters of desire as temperance, and (prudence) in matters of standing firm as courage" (*Moralia*, 441A). This text depicts Zeno setting forth the four traditional cardinal virtues—prudence, justice, temperance, and courage—and then making prudence the primary virtue by viewing the other three virtues as versions of it. The Stoic needs prudence, and not justice, temperance, or courage, to know, in any particular situation, what is the virtuous thing to do.

It might seem that Stoic ethics has little need for the kind of deliberative prudential reasoning that we saw in Socrates, Plato, and Aristotle. As we saw in chapter 3, the Stoics believe that all natural reality (*phusis*) forms a single complete whole permeated by a universal reason (*logos*) that organizes and directs it. Fortunately, this immanent *logos*, which some Stoics called a world-soul or a god, is providential—it directs everything for the best. In Stoicism, what looks like a bad thing or a tragedy is merely a part of a predetermined rational plan achieving the best possible outcome.

Although this philosophy provides great comfort for any Stoic experiencing difficulties in life it creates a challenge to the way we think about deliberation and practical reasoning in ethics. If universal reason or *logos* is directing nature then human beings really do not have to deliberate and choose one alternative from the several they could have chosen. All they need to do is read off or deduce what to do from the rational structure of nature, and then do it. Moreover, if the universal reason or *logos* is directing everything that happens, if "whatever will be, will be" thanks to its rational plan, then human beings do not have the freedom to alter anything and thus they really have no true choices to make. Whatever they do was already fated to happen anyway thanks to the universal plan governing all things.

It appears that virtuous living in Stoicism is a matter of discovering and conforming to the *a priori* norms embedded in nature, not figuring out what to do in an uncertain world, the future history of which will be shaped, at least to some extent, by human choice. The universal determinism in Stoicism would seem to undermine the possibility that humans could deliberate and then decide on a course of action knowing that they could have done otherwise, and it would seem to undermine the notion of personal responsibility as well. Yet the notions of prudence and of personal responsibility retain a major role in Stoic ethics. How can this be if everything is predetermined by the universal *logos*?

The Stoics maintain both a universal determinism governed by the *logos* and the need for prudential deliberation by insisting that the *logos* directs all beings to act in accord with their natures. Because human beings are rational by nature, the universal *logos* directs them to act "according to reason." Humans act naturally when they act rationally. Faced with a particular set of circumstances, the Stoic acts naturally by reasoning about what to do. Whatever a Stoic chooses was fated to be chosen; however, as fate always remains unknown to the chooser, he or she has to deliberate and make decisions.

The Stoic effort to harmonize human deliberation and choice in a world that is totally determined by the universal *logos* is not totally satisfactory but this is not surprising. The "free will and determinism" issue remains a notorious philosophical problem in the present day. For our purposes, however, we need to underline that the Stoics, despite their doctrine of cosmic determinism, insist on a reasoning in ethics that is truly practical, and they often call it prudence. Managing our lives requires more than theoretical knowledge of the cosmos governed by *logos*; we need to know how to make decisions about what to do and what not to do in particular situations. A text from Arius Didymus (first century B.C.E.) preserved by the fourth century Greek anthologist, John Strobaeus, gives a summary of the Stoic position.

> Prudence is the knowledge of what one should do and of what one should not do and of what is neither; it is the knowledge of what is good and of what is bad and of what is neither (good nor bad) for a natural being living in a community. (Long and Sedley, *The Hellenistic Philosophers*, 2:61H)

The Stoic idea of prudence, so understood, is not far from that of Aristotle. Although Stoic ethics is based on the predetermined rational structure of the universe the individual still has to decide what to do and how to do it in the circumstances he faces. Simply doing what is "natural" is insufficient. It is, for example, natural for living things to undergo a process of dying; however, a Stoic does not simply respond to this natural process in a passive way. Instead, the Stoic needs to decide on a course of action. Depending on the situation, he or she might decide to let nature take its course or perhaps decide to assist nature by committing suicide, a decision some prominent Stoics actually made at the end of their lives.

The Stoic norm "live according to nature" means that human beings should act according to their rational nature and deliberate about what they should do. Living "according to nature" does not mean simply accepting whatever happens naturally. Human beings have a *rational* nature and this means that they live according to their nature when they act rationally. The rational response to natural illness will vary with circumstances and with the psychological nature of the sick person. The virtuous Stoic evaluates each situation and decides which behavior will be reasonable for her given the circumstances. Sometimes prudence will even direct her to avoid perfectly natural behaviors because they would not be good in the present circumstances. Eating, for example, is natural behavior, but a reasonable Stoic today will decide not to eat when he is scheduled for surgery later in the day.

Prudence as a Skill

The Stoics, like most Greek ethicists, regarded wisdom or prudence—thus ethics—as a skill (*techne*). Aristotle, as we saw, is a notorious exception to the view that ethics is a skill. He distinguished skill and action—*techne* and *praxis*—and understood virtue ethics in terms of the latter. But the Stoics think of ethics as a skill (*techne*); in fact, they think of it as the most important skill of all, the skill of living.

The distinction between a skill and a practice is important in Aristotle because he thought that the practical reasoning employed in a skill differs in two major ways from the practical reasoning employed in action. First, the intended product in *techne* or skill restricts the field of choices available in producing it. There are only a few acceptable ways to build a good house or write a good speech, yet there are many ways to live well and achieve happiness. The person using a skill is therefore acting in a more restricted domain than the person making decisions about living life. Second, acquiring skills is largely a process of acquiring a body of knowledge about how to make a product, and that body of knowledge can be reduced in large measure to a set of instructions (*paraggelia*) that the beginner can learn from the expert. But for Aristotle, acquiring authentic virtue cannot be reduced to a set of instructions. Each situation has so many variables that the individual actually has to engage in deliberation to determine what particular action to pursue (NE 1104a4–10).

It might appear, therefore, that the Stoic perception of prudence as a skill means that their idea of prudence differs greatly from that of Aristotle, who insisted that prudence should not be confused with *techne*, the practical reasoning we use in skills. The Stoic conception of skills, however, is actually quite complex and when it is fully understood it gives a role to wisdom or prudence that is very similar to the one Aristotle gave it.

Stoics distinguish two levels of skills: those practiced by learners and those practiced by experts. This distinction runs parallel to the two kinds of action that we distinguished in chapter 3; namely, "appropriate actions" (*kathekonta*) and "right actions" (*katorthoma*). The *kathekonta* are "appropriate actions" performed by those learning how to be virtuous while the *katorthoma* are "right actions" performed by those who have become virtuous. The learner performs "appropriate actions" by following instructions while the expert performs "right actions" by following his own practical wisdom or prudence.

Skills practiced by learners are states of the soul (*hexeis*) enabling the learner to accomplish his or her objective. The learner thus performs the *appropriate* actions (*kathekonta*) and gets the job done. But skill at this level is not enough for virtue because the person practicing the virtuous skill may not be acting for the right reason. A person might not be performing the *appropriate* action for the sake of virtue but for other motives. Perhaps the motive is to win praise, or to make money, or to gain power, or to gain a reward and avoid punishment. Therefore, a person paying bills is performing an *appropriate* action in accord with justice, yet it is not a virtuous action if that person is doing it to avoid dealing with bill collectors or to enhance one's own reputation. It becomes a virtuous or *right* action only if the bills are paid because one sees that it is reasonable to do so and chooses to do it precisely because it is reasonable and thus virtuous.

Skills practiced by those who have become virtuous have something more than the skills of learners. This "something more" is the wisdom that comes with the right disposition or state of mind, what the Stoics called *diathesis*. The truly virtuous person, the person of wisdom or prudence, is the person who performs appropriate actions with the right mental state; that is, purely for the sake of virtue. Once the *appropriate* actions (*kathekonta*) are done with reason and a virtuous disposition they become *right* actions (*katorthoma*). Only the *katorthoma* are truly virtuous actions. In the words of Diogenes Laertius, writing about the Stoics probably in the third century C.E.: "Virtue is in accord with a (virtuous) disposition (*diathesis*) and is chosen for its own sake and not because of fear or hope or for the sake of any external consideration" (DL 7.89).

Prudence and the Right Disposition (*diathesis*)

Plutarch writes: "All (the Stoics) agree that virtue is a disposition (*diathesis*) of the ruling part of the soul and a power engendered by reason, or rather is itself reason (*logos*) that is consistent, firm, and unshakable" (*Moralia* 441B–C). Once one acquires the right disposition and begins performing the right actions, that person is no longer a learner but an expert; he or she has mastered the skill of living. Experts do not need a set of instructions because they can figure out how best to perform the task in the given circumstances.

In Stoic ethics, the expert is the *sophos*, the sage. The Stoic *sophos* has much in common with Aristotle's *phronimos*: both have acquired enough expertise to figure out for themselves what actions to perform in each particular situation they face. The norm for the expert is no longer the instructions that guided the apprentice; rather, it is personal wisdom. The expert is the master of the craft, and his or her wisdom exceeds the knowledge embodied in the instructions guiding the apprentice. Sextus Empiricus, writing in the second century, highlights the traditional Stoic doctrine as follows:

> Looking after one's parents and honoring them in other respects is not (by itself) the work of a virtuous person, but it is the work of a virtuous person to do this by reason of prudence. . . . Both the virtuous and those not virtuous honor their parents, but it is the mark of the wise person to honor his parents by reason of prudence, as he has the skill concerning life, which is the work of doing everything by reason of the best disposition (*diathesis*). (*Against the Professors*, 11.200–1, in Long and Sedley, *The Hellenistic Philosophers*, 2:59G)

The expert *sophos* does all things well by acting according to right reason (*kata logon orthon*) and virtue (*kata areten*). The *sophos*, according to Diogenes Laertius, enjoys complete autonomy in determining what response in any situation is virtuous: "And all things belong to the wise because they (the Stoics) say that the law has given them absolute authority (*pantele exousian*)" (DL 7.125). While it is not clear from the text just what "law"

Diogenes has in mind here, it is probably the law of Zeus, which some early Stoics, most notably Chrysippus, identified with the *logos* that governs everything in the world. The text does indicate that the law or *logos* governing all things bestows on the wise an absolute authority in acting. The law does not dictate to the sage what is virtuous; rather, the law authorizes the *sophos* to determine, through use of personal wisdom, what should be done. In this way, the prudence of the *sophos* in Stoicism plays a role similar to the prudence of the *phronimos* in Aristotle.

The prudence of the Stoic *sophos* is sensitive to context and circumstances, as was the prudence of the Aristotelian *phronimos*. The *sophos* does not follow laws; instead, he or she evaluates the situation and determines what is reasonable. Thus, Diogenes tells us, a sage (*sophos*) might decide to enter politics in order to restrain vice and promote virtue. However, the sage will only seek political authority if the circumstances are right. A sage might even decide that it is reasonable to break strong natural taboos—perhaps behaving as a cannibal and eating human flesh in some circumstances (*kata peristasin*; DL 7.121).

Achieving authentic wisdom is not easy and perhaps only a few can become authentic Stoic sages. But this does not change the ethical doctrine: only the wise have authentic virtue and they become truly virtuous by assessing the situation and deciding what will be virtuous given the circumstances. Prudence is the norm for making decisions once a person has obtained wisdom. The rest of us, beginners or apprentices in learning the skills of living, will have to rely on rules and instructions unless and until we acquire the wisdom and expertise to manage our own lives as do the sages.

The frequent Stoic use of the word *episteme* (science) in relation to virtue should not mislead us into thinking that Stoic ethics is some kind of universal scientific knowledge rather than a practical skill (*techne*) pertaining to particular actions in particular situations. While it is true that Aristotle made sharp distinctions between *episteme* and both *phronesis* and *techne*, and did not use the former term for practical deliberation, the Stoics made no such distinction. For them, *episteme* is the word for knowledge in the domain of ethics as well as in the other domains of great interest to them—physics and logic. And *sophia* is the word often used for practical and deliberative reasoning as well as for theoretical and deductive reasoning.

When the Stoics talk about reasoning in ethics, they use both the words *episteme* and *phronesis*. *Episteme* in ethics for the Stoics, however, means the same kind of practical reasoning that we associate with *phronesis*. Their interest is practical—discerning a good life and figuring out what actions will achieve it in whatever cir cumstances we face. Once one has become skillful, that person has the expertise to choose wisely what will be a good move without relying on the instructions. This expert knowledge is the best one can achieve, and the Stoics often call it *episteme* as well as *phronesis*.

There is one important difference, however, between the Stoic *sophos* and the Aristotelian *phronimos*. The Stoic expert is never wrong; his or her knowledge is infallible in the sense that it inevitably succeeds in making the sage virtuous and thus in bringing happiness. This is why the Stoic sage is stoical in the face of tragedy. Tragedy cannot touch such a person because acting virtuously, if one has achieved wisdom, guarantees happiness for the *sophos*. On the other hand, Aristotle's *phronimos* or prudent person has no such guarantee. Although acting virtuously gives one the best chance of happiness, tragedy can overwhelm the happiness of even the most virtuous of lives.

Prudence in Panaetius

One helpful example of how the Stoics conceived of prudence and deliberation is found in Cicero's *De Officiis* where Cicero is explaining the work of Panaetius, a second century Stoic from Rhodes. Panaetius (185–110 B.C.E.) led the Stoic school from 129 to 110. His book *On the Appropriate Thing* (*Peri Kathekontos*) was the major source for Cicero's book titled *De Officiis*. Regrettably, only fragments of Panaetius's work survive so we have to rely on Cicero's exposition for his views.

Panaetius held, as did all Stoics, that we achieve virtue and happiness by "living according to nature." Human nature, however, is a complex notion and Panaetius distinguished four major aspects of it. Cicero tells us that these four different aspects of nature result in our having four natural roles in life. (The Latin word for "role" here is *persona*; it literally translates as "mask" and originally connoted the different roles an actor performed in a stage play). Two of these roles, the second and the fourth, show clearly the foundational role of deliberation and prudence in the Stoic ethics of Panaetius.

Our first natural role springs from the common rational nature we all share. This role sets us apart from animals and is the source of what is generally appropriate (*kathekon*) and decorous for us as human beings (*De Officiis* I, 107).

Our second natural role springs from the particular physical and psychological characteristics that are unique to each of us (*De Officiis* I, 107). This role sets us apart from each other and is the source of what is specifically appropriate and decorous for each of us as individuals. The Stoic aphorism "live according to nature" thus understands nature in both a general and a particular sense. We should act according to our common rational nature and also according to our unique individual nature.

The importance of each person's unique nature is paramount in Stoic decision making. Cicero illustrates this with a life and death example—figuring out whether or not to commit suicide. The decision for a Stoic depends in large measure on the particular nature of the individual contemplating suicide. Depending on the person's particular nature, the suicide could be reasonable or not reasonable. To see this, imagine two virtuous people in identical circumstances and facing the last stages of terminal illness. In a rule-based ethics two conclusions are possible: the rule would either allow both persons to commit suicide or it would prohibit both from committing suicide. In Stoicism, however, a third conclusion is possible: the suicide of one could be reasonable and moral while the suicide of the other could be unreasonable and immoral.

The difference can be traced to the different specific natures of the two people. Virtuous people will act "according to nature," yet "nature" embraces a person's particular human nature as well as one's general humanity. So the question becomes: is it in accord with my *particular* nature to commit suicide in this situation? And here one Stoic *sophos* might deliberate and decide that suicide truly accords with his particular nature while another *sophos* could reach the opposite conclusion in the same set of circumstances. Both are right—for themselves. People can reach different decisions about what to do because their particular natures differ. The decision to commit suicide is not based on nature as universal but on the particular nature of the individual. Hence, all else being equal, suicide can be virtuous for one person but not for another (*De Officiis* I, 112).

Thus Stoicism, at least in the view of Panaetius as reported by Cicero, stresses the particularity involved in "acting according to nature." We all share the same rational nature, but, in addition, each of us has a particular unique nature, and our decisions should accord with our particular natures as well as our general nature as human beings. To live according to nature, Panaetius and Cicero remind us, is to live according to both the universal and the particular facets of our nature. And even if a certain course of action would be, objectively speaking, greater and better, a person should nonetheless judge one's endeavors by the pattern or "rule" (*regula*) of one's particular nature: "We regulate our endeavors by the rule of our own particular nature" (*De Officiis* I, 110). Nothing that goes "against the grain" of our particular natural abilities and tendencies is fitting for us to pursue (*De Officiis* I, 110). Every person, therefore, should evaluate one's own nature with its unique assets and liabilities, and then rely on prudence (*prudentia*) in the same way that wise actors choose not the best plays but the plays most suitable for their particular skills (*De Officiis* I, 114).

Panaetius identified two other natural roles in addition to the two roles that we have just discussed. The third natural role that we play in life originates in luck, both good and bad. This role is dictated by fortune and misfortune, which might bestow or destroy health, wealth, and so forth. There is not much we can do about luck except to accept it—stoically.

The fourth and final natural role, however, again shows the importance of individualized practical wisdom. This role is the role we play in life. In addition to deliberation about individual actions, we need to decide who and what kind of person we want to be and what kind of life we want to lead. This is something we assume by "our own choice" (*nostra voluntate*; *De Officiis* I, 115) and, says Cicero, this is the most difficult deliberation (*deliberatio*) of all (*De Officiis* I, 117).

Cicero's account clearly shows how Panaetius thought that virtue requires prudential deliberation. Each person has to figure out whether an action—even the radical action of suicide—is in accord with one's own particular natural constitution and with the role one has chosen to play in life. There is no rule saying a person should commit or not commit suicide in a particular situation. Each person, mindful of one's own physical and psychological nature, figures that out for herself. And each person also deliberates about all his free choices and about how to order life as a whole, given one's innate natural tendencies (*De Officiis* I, 119). Despite the universality of reason permeating all nature and shared by all humans in a special way, then, each Stoic still has to deliberate and to rely on prudence to know what actions and what calling to pursue in life.

The Stoic Sage *(sophos)*

What we learn from this review is that the Greek Stoic ethicists, despite some real differences of opinion, nonetheless made the controlling virtue in virtue ethics the intellectual virtue of practical wisdom or prudence. Certainly, the virtuous person will be temperate, just, caring, kind, loving, courageous, and so forth, but it is prudence that tells her just what is virtuous in any situation.

Thus in Stoic virtue ethics the ideal in life is not to be a just person, or a loving person, or a kind person, or a courageous person, but a wise person, a *sophos*. Stoicism echoes here the now familiar themes of earlier virtue ethics. The virtues of justice and love do not tell us how to live; prudence does that. The virtues in our lives depend on the decisions we make, and the decision-making virtue is prudence. Acting for the sake of moral laws and principles will not make us authentically virtuous. We become virtuous by achieving maturity, thanks to education and moral training, which will enable us to manage our own lives so they will be good lives.

The Stoics, unlike Plato and Aristotle, felt that every normally functioning human being actually has the potential to develop their practical reasoning and achieve authentic virtue and happiness. The Stoic insistence that everyone has the potential for virtue and happiness leads them to several important conclusions. One conclusion is that every person in the world is worthy of respect because every person has the potential of becoming a sage. Stoic ethics thus anticipates a widespread contemporary theme in ethics: respect for all human beings. It makes no fundamental difference whether the person is a citizen or a noncitizen, male or female, slave or free, rich or poor, sick or healthy; respect is due because we are all equal in the sense that we all have a rational soul allowing us the autonomy to become virtuous. Reason is the foundation of human dignity because by it we can do what no other being can do— manage our own lives by deliberating and deciding how to cope with our lot in life.

A second conclusion is the implication that people are not only citizens of their city or empire, but also citizens of the world. Hence the political order is not, as many think, simply local; instead, it is international. The Stoics thus began a thinking still under way today: some kind of international law and judicial system, as well as some kind of international language, perhaps the language of human rights, is needed to provide environments where people can achieve virtue.

As important as both these implications are the general Stoic approach to living a good life is not without problems. First, the Stoic can claim more easily than Aristotle that everyone has the power to achieve happiness in life because they defined happiness narrowly. In Stoicism, happiness consists of virtue, and virtue alone. Acquiring virtue is the only good, and losing virtue the only evil. Thus the loss of a loved one, or the lack of liberty, health, wealth, or education, is never something bad for a Stoic sage. Virtue, and virtue alone, is sufficient for happiness even if you suffer great tragedy or happen to live as a disenfranchised slave.

Second, while everyone has the potential for happiness the state of Stoic virtue is so difficult to achieve that few can actually do it. Remember, the Stoics believe that the major causes of unhappiness in life are passions and feelings, and their response was to root them out so that only reason remains. But few people can do that; in fact, few people would ever want to do that. Feelings run deep in human life and one cannot help but wonder how many followers of Stoicism have actually rooted out the passions and achieved virtue. Despite the Stoic tendency to acknowledge that everyone has the potential for virtue and happiness, their insistence that virtue means rooting out all emotional attachments strikes many as an effort not according to but contrary to human nature.

Finally, some of their political doctrines strike us as bizarre. The Stoics were more radical thinkers than either Plato or Aristotle, and they often challenged widely accepted positions. Both Zeno and Chrysippus wrote books with the title *Republic*; unfortunately they no longer exist. Comments from later authors indicate, however, that these works advocated sharing wives and the wearing of revealing clothing that exposes all parts of the body (*DL* 7.33). They also tolerated incest (Plutarch, *Moralia,* 1044F) and cannibalism (Sextus Empiricus, *Outlines of Pyrrhonism* 3.247, in Long and Sedley, *The Hellenistic Philosophers,* 2:67G). The fact that such great Stoics as Zeno and Chrysippus advocated sharing wives or "swinging" and accepted incest and cannibalism as moral possibilities casts a troubling shadow on their ability to reason prudently. Yet their *doctrine* of practical reasoning is not thereby destroyed. Later Stoics eventually concluded, thanks to practical reasoning, that these behaviors are not conducive to virtue, and rejected them.

One of the attractive features of a virtue ethics based on practical reason or prudence is its self-correcting learning process capable of reversing positions once an alternative is seen as more reasonable; that is, as more conducive to virtue and a good life. The major insight of Stoicism—that only good intentions and prudential decision making create the right actions (*katorthomata*) that constitute authentic virtue, which is the essence of happiness—has an enduring attraction. No action reflecting a character virtue is authentic unless it comes "from the heart" or, as the Stoic might say, from the right intention (*diathesis*) and unless it conforms to "right reason." Intelligent personal decision making and the commitment to do what is done for the sake of virtue are what create virtue in our lives, and virtue, for the Stoic sage, guarantees a happy life.

Glossary

action (*praxis*). Broadly speaking, an action is what we do. The verb for doing something is *prattein*. More strictly, *praxis* is what we do deliberately. Ethics is a *practical* reasoning because it is about *praxis*, what we do deliberately.

appropriate action (*kathekon*). This participial form of the verb *katheko* indicates what is fitting and proper. Stoics usually used the word in the plural (*ta kathekonta*) to indicate actions that are appropriate for a human being to perform. They contrasted these with *ta katorthoma,* which are a subset of appropriate actions—the *right* actions. Only right actions are truly virtuous. A person who is kind to his or her parents performs *appropriate actions*; however, they are not *right actions* unless he or she performs them for the right reasons. Acts of kindness performed to enhance one's reputation or to gain the inheritance, for example, are appropriate actions but they are not right or virtuous actions. In later writers (toward the first century B.C.E.), *kathekon* acquired the notion of duty—it is not only proper for children to take care of their parents, it is their duty. Cicero translated *kathekonta* into Latin as *officia*, duties. The original Stoic idea, however, did not so much connote duty as the appropriateness of actions regardless of whether or not they were performed for the right reason.

character (*ethos*). The best translation of *ethos* (spelled with a long "e") is probably moral character or simply character. Character is related to habit (*ethos* spelled with a short "e") but it is not the same. Both habits and character can be good or bad. Good character is acquired in two stages. The preliminary stage occurs during childhood when others direct us toward good feelings and actions; however, authentic good character does not emerge until a person begins making his or her own decisions to seek what is good for its own sake. Repeated good decisions coalesce into enduring states that can be identified as character virtues, virtues such as justice, temperance, and so forth. Thus, deliberately chosen good actions create the virtuous states that form good character.

decision making (*prohairesis*). Good decision making requires (1) recognizing some goal that is good to pursue, (2) deliberating about how to achieve this good, and (3) deciding what is to be done and then executing that decision. Decision making (*prohairesis*) is not the same as choice (*hairesis*); we can choose something at random while decision making always includes deliberation or practical reasoning. Excellence in decision making is the excellence known as the virtue of prudence.

deliberation (*boule*). A key element of prudence, deliberation is the rational consideration about how to achieve a goal. In virtue ethics, the goal is happiness and deliberation is figuring out how to achieve it. Sometimes it appears that a virtuous person, what Aristotle calls a *phronimos*, makes a prudent decision without any deliberation. In such cases, Aristotle insists, the deliberation has occurred in the past and allowed decision making expertise to develop. Once expertise has been acquired the virtuous person does not repeat the process of deliberation when analogous situations arise. Aristotle speaks of *euboulia*, which is "good deliberation." Good deliberation is deliberation about the right thing, in the right way, and at the right time so that the goal of happiness and living a good life can be achieved.

desire (*orexis*). This is the general word for all kinds of striving or yearning for something. The word "conation" would be a good translation if it were not so rarely used in English. Desires can be irrational cravings and urges for what is pleasant as well as rational strivings for something not pleasant but perceived as truly good, such as going to the dentist. Desires are the wellsprings of human action; they set us in motion. Greek ethics is based on the good that human beings desire above all else—a life of happiness.

end (*telos*). The end is the natural or designed goal of an organism or of a fabricated thing. The goal of a living organism is to function well and thereby to live well; the goal or purpose of a thing is what it is designed to do. The complete and overriding end for humans is called happiness—living well and doing well.

ethics (*ethica*, spelled with a long "e"). We achieve happiness in life by developing a virtuous character (*ethos*, spelled with a long "e"). We develop a virtuous character from the habits (the word for habit is *ethos*, spelled with a short "e") that are the result of reasonable (prudential) decisions. The word *ethica* is a neuter plural adjective used as a substantive and literally means something like "ethical matters." From Aristotle, we have two ethical studies—the *Ethica Nicomacheia* and the *Ethica Eudemia*. These books could be translated as the *Nicomachean Treatise on Ethical Matters* and the *Eudemian Treatise on Ethical Matters*. Zeno also wrote a book titled *Ethica,* and Chrysippus wrote numerous ethical treatises, including one titled *Ethical Theses* (*Theseis Ethicai*), but none of these books survive. Although the adjective "ethical" in these titles denotes the study of virtuous character, it is also the study of prudential decision making since we acquire virtuous character only by deliberately deciding to act according to right reason or prudence. Hence, the ethical treatises are not only about the character virtues such as justice and love but also about the intellectual virtue that produces the authentic character virtues—prudence.

feeling (*pathos*). The word *pathos* is derived from the verb *paschein,* which means to be affected in some way. Words such as "feelings," "emotions," and "passions" describe our being affected—these feelings just come over us and affect our whole experience of life. Among the major feelings are fear, anger, love, distress, pity, and grief. The ethical debate is what to do about our feelings, emotions, and passions. Plato and Aristotle advocate guiding and moderating them with reason; the Stoics, on the other hand, recommend rooting them out because they mislead reason.

friendship (*philia*). This term covers a multitude of virtuous interpersonal relationships ranging from the love among husbands, wives, children, and close friends, to commercial and political friendships among virtuous people. It does not appear on the short list of Socratic and Platonic virtues; however, Aristotle lists it as a major character virtue and treats it more extensively than any of the other virtues, devoting two of the ten books in the *Nicomachean Ethics* to it. He describes love as a relationship wherein two virtuous people are truly fond of each other and each is devoted to doing good for the other for the sake of the other, and not for any pleasure or utilitarian gain they might achieve through the relationship.

function (*ergon*). Although the word has many meanings, the central idea is "what something does." Both living and nonliving things function in various ways. In ethics, a person achieves happiness when he or she functions in a reasonable or appropriate way. The idea of appropriate (*oikeios*) function gained credence in Stoicism and led to the concept of *oikeiosis* or "appropriation" whereby the appropriate way to act is "according to nature."

god, gods (*theos, theoi*). The philosophers often speak of god or gods and use the term loosely. Usually the term refers to the gods of Greek antiquity—Zeus and the others—who were the objects of worship, prayer, and sacrifice, and in whose honor temples were built. However, these gods were the gods of myth (*muthos*) and the philosophical emphasis on reason (*logos*) was bound to generate questions about, and criticisms of, the older mythical religious practices. One such example is the opening (and only surviving) sentence of the Sophist Protagoras's book *About the Gods*: "About the gods I cannot say either that they exist or that they do not exist, for many things hinder knowing them, the uncertainty of the matter and the fact that man's life is short" (*DL* 9.52). Enraged at this agnostic challenge, the Athenians expelled the foreigner Protagoras from their city and burnt the copies of his book. Several decades later the Athenians executed one of their own, Socrates, after charging him with rejecting the gods of the city. Plato, Aristotle, and Epicurus were more circumspect when they wrote about the gods of the city—Plato even suggested in the *Laws* that the Nocturnal Council should punish atheism. Aristotle accepted the religious practices of his adopted city, but, in the *Physics* and *Metaphysics*, he also developed a theoretical theology of an eternal immaterial unmoved mover (he sometimes spoke of unmoved movers) called god who would not be the object of religious practice because he neither knew nor cared about what happens in the human realm. In his *Letter to Menoeceus*, Epicurus insisted that the existence of the immortal and blessed gods is self-evident but that most popular beliefs about them are misleading and false. Neither Aristotle nor Epicurus think that the gods act in human history. The Stoics had a different idea. As Diogenes Laertius reports (*DL* 7.147), they tend to make god an immortal perfect being without any evil who is the craftsman (*demiourgos*) as well as a providential father, and who is known by different names such as Zeus, Athena, Hera, Poseidon, and so forth. Zeus either directs the Stoic *logos* (reason) that governs the world or is identical with it. This leads to a kind of pantheism and materialism because the Stoics often speak of the *logos* permeating nature as breath or fire.

good (*agathos*). Simply put, something is good if it actually functions well or can function well. Thus, a tool or an animal is good if it functions well. In ethics, a person has a good life if she is functioning well. Functioning well for a human being means living well, living a good life, living a life of fulfillment, what the Greeks called happiness. In the plural, "goods" (*ta agatha*) is often used to denote the things that constitute or contribute to living well. All agree that the virtues are such goods, some (most notably Aristotle) insist that other nonvirtuous goods are needed as well if a life is to be truly good.

habit (*ethos*, short e). Both animals and humans acquire habits by repetition and training based on the dynamics of pleasure and pain. Moral training and education instill good habits in children and these become the natural character virtues that serve as the platform for the autonomous decision making that creates the authentic character virtues, and these form the person's good character—his *ethos* (long e).

happiness (*eudaimonia*). The greatest human good is living a life that is a good life, and the word for this is happiness. The root meaning is *eu-daimon* or good fate, having a good lot in life. Unlike the earlier authors of the tragedies, the philosophers taught that having a good life is a fate that is largely if not totally up to us. Happiness is living well and doing well over time. All the philosophers claim that virtue is a necessary component of happiness. Some, the Stoics, for example, claim that virtue is all we need.

justice (*dikaiosune*). The philosophers often speak of justice as a political state whereby the various parts of a city-state are coordinated so they achieve the common good and allow citizens to live good lives. Such a society would be a just society. Justice is also a personal state and one of the character virtues. Plato views the personal virtue of justice as the virtue that harmonizes the three parts of the soul just as social justice harmonizes the three classes in the *Republic*. Aristotle notes that personal justice has two meanings. "Complete" justice describes a person with all the virtues, much as today we might call someone a person of integrity, while "particular" justice describes the specific character virtue of that name. The virtue of particular justice in turn has two aspects: distributive justice means the person takes from the community only what he deserves and corrective justice means the person can recover what he might have lost through injustice. The Stoics also spoke of the personal virtue of justice in distributive terms: Zeno said that justice is prudence in matters of distribution based on merit.

law (*nomos*). The word law is somewhat ambivalent because it means informal but widely accepted practices in a community as well as formal legislation and regulation. *Nomos* is something that originates by human convention that may or may not be formalized in written laws. *Nomos* is sharply opposed to *phusis* which refers to what is established by nature and not by culture, although the gap between law and nature began to close with the Stoic emphasis on the *logos* (but not the *nomos*) permeating all nature, including human nature. Only with Cicero and Philo of Alexandria in the first century B.C.E. do we see the notion of "natural law" or "law of nature" emerging. These phrases would have been an oxymoron for the earlier philosophers, who made a sharp distinction between nature and convention, *phusis* and *nomos*.

luck (*tuche*). Before the philosophers, the Greeks attributed happiness or unhappiness in life mostly to luck, fate, or chance. Luck or fortune doles out our lot in life and there is not much that we can do about it. The philosophers insisted that we can do something about achieving happiness if we acquire the ability to develop virtue. Most of them called this ability a skill (*techne*) and thus opposed *techne* to *tuche*. The exception is Aristotle, who confined skills to making things and called the practical reasoning that overcomes luck prudence.

nature (*physis*). The structure and function of anything is its nature. Every class of beings has its natural constitution and tendency toward an appropriate end or goal; this comprises its nature apart from any human intervention. Nature is thus distinguished from nurture, which pertains to *nomos*. Virtue ethics originates in human nature, more specifically the natural human desire to achieve the goal of living well, which is the criterion for what makes a life successful.

perception (*aisthesis*). Although perception often refers to the operation of any one of our five senses, in ethics it connotes the awareness of particular features in any situation that are morally relevant. It plays a major role in virtue ethics because prudence focuses not on general principles and rules but on the particular elements in a situation that are morally significant for achieving happiness. We need to perceive both the particular facts and the salient moral factors or values in each situation we face in order to make good decisions.

the political (*e politike*). The word *politike* is a feminine singular adjective that Aristotle often uses as a substantive—the political, *e politike*. It is related to citizenship or government (*politeia*) and citizen (*polites*). What might be the unexpressed feminine singular noun that Aristotle has in mind when he uses the adjective "political?" Most translations and commentaries suggest that it is "*episteme*" (science) and translate *e politike* as "political science." Yet Aristotle does not speak of *politike episteme* and usually reserves the word "science" for theoretical and not practical knowledge. The more likely unexpressed noun supporting the adjective "political" is *phronesis* (prudence). Aristotle says (NE 1041b23–1142a11) that prudence, although it is usually thought to pertain to how an individual manages his or her personal life, actually embraces three other areas of life: household management (*e oikonomia*), legislation (*e nomothesia*), and "the political" (*e politike*). And he further divides the political into two kinds, "the deliberative" (*e bouleutike*) and "the judicial" (*e dikastike*). Following this text the phrase *e politike* would not mean "political science" but "political prudence." However, political prudence, along with other practices such as medical practice and athletic coaching, does rely on a body of general knowledge relevant to its field and thus can be called a science in a wide sense (NE 1180b13–29). According to Aristotle "the political" (political prudence setting up a society with good laws to educate and orient people toward virtue) is the necessary condition for "the ethical" (personal prudence creating virtuous character). The actual title of Aristotle's book known as the *Politics* is *Politica,* which is the neuter plural of the adjective *politikos* and literally means something like "political things." A good translation might be "Treatise on Political Matters." The Greek title of Plato's book known as the *Republic* is *Politeia* (Government), and the title of his *Statesman* is *Politikos.* Both Zeno and Chrysippus also wrote lost books with the title *Politeia.*

principle (*arche*). In modern ethics, principle or principles have two major meanings. In the first meaning, principles are derived from moral theories and serve as guides for action. In American bioethics, for example, there is a long tradition of proposing such action-guiding principles as autonomy, beneficence, justice, and nonmaleficence. The second modern meaning makes principle the starting point that gives rise to a moral theory. Thus, Bentham (in *An Introduction to the Principles of Morals and Legislation*) and Mill (in *Utilitarianism*) speak of "the principle of utility" as the foundation of morality, while Kant (in the *Metaphysical Elements of Justice*) makes the categorical imperative the "supreme basic principle of moral philosophy." For the Greeks principles have only the latter meaning—they are starting points for reasoning. In ethics, the starting point is the fact that human beings are beings seeking happiness; that is, a life that goes well. Personal happiness is the starting point of Greek ethics, and their ethical philosophies are attempts to elaborate accounts of how to achieve this goal.

prudence (*phronesis*). This is the word most often used by the philosophers to describe the intelligent deliberation that supports good decision making and thus promotes the person's happiness by creating the authentic character virtues that are crucial components of a good life. Prudence is a practical reasoning that dictates the right way to act in the particular situation and thus requires a perception that grasps the unique circumstances in each situation. Until a person begins acting on the basis of his or her own prudential reasoning, that person is not truly virtuous and not living a truly good life. Prudential reasoning requires an awareness of life's most important goal (happiness) and relies on some general knowledge about what is good or bad for a good life, but it is primarily the ability to figure out in each situation what move will likely promote personal happiness and a good life.

reason (*logos*). This is a widely used word with many shades of meaning. It is derived from *lego*, to speak, and conveys the general notion of bringing order out of chaos by thinking and speaking. Plato contrasted *logos* and *mythos*, rational explanations and mythical accounts. In ethics Aristotle often uses *logos* to indicate the process of prudential human reasoning, and insists that the ethical norm is acting "according to the right reasoning" (*kata ton orthon logon*) where the right reasoning is clearly prudential deliberation and not deductive scientific reasoning. The Stoics, returning to a thought first expressed by Heraclitus, had conceived of *logos* not only as a rational ability in humans but as the rational organizing principle of all reality. All nature is permeated and governed by this universal providential *logos,* which is sometimes considered divine.

science (*episteme*). This word has both wide and narrow meanings. In the wide sense, *episteme* indicates any organized body of natural knowledge. The practice of medicine, rhetoric, legislation, and military strategy are thus sciences in the wide sense. In one narrow sense, as defined by Plato in the *Republic*, *episteme* refers only to the grasp of transcendent realities such as mathematical entities and the Forms. Another narrow sense is defined by Aristotle in Book VI of the *Nicomachean Ethics,* where *episteme* refers to the theoretical reasoning that is found in physics, mathematics, and what we call metaphysics and is contrasted with the practical reasoning that we call skill (*techne*) and prudence (*phronesis*). Often, philosophers, including Plato and Aristotle, use the word *episteme* in a rather wide sense to indicate rational (as opposed to mythical) knowledge.

skill (*techne*). Other possible translations of this word are "craft" and "art." Skills include making and painting the famous Athenian *kraters* (bowls), constructing buildings and ships, sculpting statues, crafting speeches (rhetoric), writings plays, and so forth. Most Greek philosophers (the notable exception is Aristotle) consider ethics a *techne*—the acquired *techne* of knowing how to live a happy life in whatever situation faces us. A person with ethical *techne* is the person with the acquired skill of living well, the person who knows how to craft a successful and good life.

soul (*psyche*). This is a word with a long and complicated history of meanings. An important source of ideas about the soul for Socrates and Plato was the Pythagorean doctrine of a soul that survives death by entering another body. Plato gradually developed the idea that the human soul is an immaterial self-moving mover of the body that can exist independently of its body and, in fact, is not only immortal but eternal. In the *Republic,* he developed his famous threefold division of the soul into its appetitive, spirited, and rational parts. Aristotle also viewed the human soul as an immaterial mover of the body but considered it a nonmoving mover because it moves as a final cause, and final causes of motion need not be in motion themselves to move others (a glass of water need not move to attract a thirsty person toward it). Aristotle's human soul moves the body by thought, desire, and decision. It is also the formal cause of a human being (the body is the material cause) but it does not survive the death of the body, which is the dissolution of the human being understood as a composition of matter (the body) and form (the soul). The word soul had a variety of meanings for the Stoics but generally they moved away from viewing it as immaterial and often identified it with the air or breath (*pneuma*) in the body. A person thus acquires a human soul with the first breath and loses it when he stops breathing. This view is similar to the ancient Semitic view, which holds that meaningful human life begins at birth and ends at death, and is a reminder that Zeno, the founder of Stoicism, came from the large Semitic community on Cyprus. The materiality of the soul allows us to understand more easily the Stoic doctrine that the soul is the seat of passions and feelings as well as thought—the soul is not an immaterial entity or faculty but the air in the body. Despite their talk about reason and the *logos*, the Stoics were materialists. The rational soul in the human body is air and the rational soul or *logos* governing the world is a cosmic breath or fire pervading the whole world.

state (*hexis*). The word is derived from *exo*, the future of *echo*, which means having something. *Hexis* is something I have that affects my future. This something is an enduring condition of my body or mind acquired by repetition. A common translation of *hexis* is habit, but Aristotle often used *hexis* to designate authentic character virtue, which confines the meaning to a particular class of habits—the good habits acquired by deliberate choice, which form my character as a person of virtue.

temperance (*sophrosune*). This is the character virtue associated with reasonableness or moderation in satisfying our appetites for food, fluids, sex, and drugs (which usually meant wine for the Greeks). In a wider sense, the word designates reason and intelligence in all things, and thus comes close to the intellectual virtue of prudence.

virtue (*arete*). Although virtue in a wide sense means any kind of excellence in the more narrow moral sense it refers to a person's excellence as a human being. The word virtue occasionally designates personal excellence itself and sometimes it designates specific aspects of personal excellence such as justice, temperance, love, endurance (courage), wisdom, prudence, and so forth. The specific aspects of excellence—the virtues—are the affective and intellectual states that make a life excellent. Children acquire a preliminary stage of these states by character education, training, and good laws; adults, however, acquire true excellence only by personally making decisions in accord with right reason—that is, practical wisdom or prudence. There is no adjective corresponding to virtue in Greek. They did not speak of a virtuous person, or of a virtuous action, or of a virtuous character, although *aristos*, which is the superlative form of *agathos* (the adjective "good") and means "best," shares the same etymological root as *arete*.

wisdom (*sophia*). The general word for wisdom is *sophia*. Most philosophers did not clearly distinguish between practical wisdom and theoretical wisdom or science, but the contexts usually make it clear which kind of wisdom they intend. Aristotle, however, did clearly distinguish between *sophia* and *phronesis*.

Selected Greek Virtue Ethicists

Aristotle (384–322). Unlike Socrates and Plato, Aristotle was not an Athenian citizen. He was born at Stagira in Thrace, a region in northern Greece near Macedonia. He came to Athens about 368 and studied at the Academy until Plato's death in 347. When Plato's nephew became head of the Academy, he left Athens, married Pythias, and they had a daughter. In 343, Philip of Macedon invited Aristotle to tutor his son, Alexander. When the young Alexander succeeded his assassinated father in 336, Aristotle returned to Athens and founded his own school, the Lyceum. After Pythias died, he shared his home with Herpyllis and fathered a son, Nicomachus, who may have edited the famous *Nicomachean Ethics.* Shortly after Alexander's death, anti-Macedonian sentiment was on the rise, forcing Aristotle to leave Athens for a family estate on an island, where he died in 322, leaving a will that provided for Herpyllis and their son. Although he also wrote dialogues for the general public, only fragments survive. Fortunately, many of his scholarly works in logic, philosophy of nature, ethics, rhetoric, politics, and literary criticism do survive thanks in large part to the editorial work of Andronicus of Rhodes in the first century B.C.E. Aristotle was the first to produce treatises devoted to ethics and to him we owe the idea that "ethics" is not simply a way of living and acting but a field worthy of academic study.

Chrysippus (280–207). After Cleanthes, who succeeded Zeno as head of the Stoic school, died, Chrysippus took over and became the most influential thinker during its Greek (pre-Roman) history. He wrote scores of books, though none survive. Fortunately, his ideas, which often advance and organize the doctrines of Zeno and

Cleanthes, are discussed at length by others. He introduced a strong version of the unity of the virtues that became standard in Stoicism after him: not only does having one virtue mean the person has them all but every *action* a virtuous person performs involves all the virtues as well. A just action is thus also an action that is courageous, temperate, prudent, pious, and so forth.

Cicero (106–43). Cicero is obviously not a Greek virtue ethicist; in fact, he was neither Greek nor a philosopher. But he is important for being among the first to translate the Greek ideas into Latin, which was to become the language of philosophy for the next seventeen centuries. As a young man, Cicero attended the lectures of several leading Greek philosophers (Phaedrus the Epicurean, Diodotus the Stoic, and Philo, who represented the tradition at Plato's Academy). He later studied philosophy at Athens and Rhodes. He was actively involved in Roman legal and political life, serving as prosecutor, defense lawyer, consul in the Senate, and governor of Cilicia. When Caesar became dictator in 47, Cicero left his post in Cilicia and returned to one of his estates near Rome, where he devoted the remaining years of his life to writing. His translations sometimes pushed philosophical concepts in new directions. For example, he translated the Stoic notion of *kathekon* as *officium*, and thus "what is appropriate" became "what is a duty." And he translated *arete* (excellence) as *virtus* (virtue). And the Stoic idea of reason directing all of nature (*logos phuseos*) became for Cicero a law directing nature (*lex naturalis*), that is, "natural law." Cicero's Latin terminology was a great influence on subsequent European thought, especially as Greek was forgotten and Latin became the dominant language. A political assassination ended his life.

Cleanthes (330–232). After Zeno died, Cleanthes became the head of the Stoic school about 262. He is the author of the most famous theistic text of the Greek Stoics, the *Hymn to Zeus,* wherein Zeus is praised as the one who directs the universal reason (the *logos*) that governs all things. None of his works survive.

Epicurus (341–270). Born at Samos, Epicurus came to Athens and eventually opened his own school in the walled garden of an estate about 306. Most of his writings were lost although some fragments and several letters survive. His central academic concern was ethics—the study of how one could achieve a good human life, which he described as a life lived without suffering and troubles. He insisted that ethical discussions, no less than any other endeavor, are worthless unless they actually help reduce the anxieties and troubles that we experience in living. He is generally known, and frequently criticized, as a hedonist but his hedonism advocates finding happiness by living a peaceful and serene life.

Plato (428–348). Plato came from an upper-class Athenian family. A pupil of Socrates, he founded his famous Academy in 388. The curriculum included astronomy, physical science, and mathematics as well as philosophy. Unfortunately, Plato's lectures have been lost, though we have about two dozen of the dialogues he prepared for the general public. Socrates plays a key role in these dialogues, probably speaking for himself in the early works and probably serving as spokesperson for Plato's ideas in the later works. Although Plato spent most of his time at the Academy, he did make several voyages to Sicily before his death in Athens in 348.

Socrates (479–399). In his youth, Socrates studied various natural philosophies at Athens. Growing impatient with the irresolvable disagreements among the various theories, he then turned from natural philosophy to the study of how a person can best live his or her life. He was married to Xanthippe and had three sons, one of whom was quite young when he died. He served with honor in the military during the Peloponnesian War and generally avoided serving in Athenian political life, although he was selected by lot in 406 to serve on a judicial board that presided over a famous trial of ten generals accused of abandoning survivors in a naval battle. It is impossible to know what Socrates actually taught because none of his own writings survive. He often appears as a speaker in Plato's dialogues, but Plato, especially after his first dialogues, is obviously using Socrates as a literary character to express his own doctrines. To complicate matters even more, Plato's admiration for Socrates appears exaggerated when we read Xenophon, who presents a more mundane and critical picture. Socrates was brought to trial under a restored democratic regime in 399. He was accused of two vague charges: not honoring the gods of the city and corrupting the youth. The jury found him guilty and then, under Athenian law, its members had to choose either the penalty proposed by the prosecution or one proposed by the guilty party. The prosecution asked for the death penalty and seventy-year-old Socrates, instead of asking for a fine, prison, or even exile, proposed a rather bizarre alternative "punishment" that antagonized many jurors—free meals for life in the city hall dining room! Upset at what they perceived as arrogance, the majority of the jury opted for the prosecution's recommendation and Socrates was sentenced to die. Several weeks later he drank the hemlock. Two of his students offered radically different interpretations of his rather unusual behavior during the trial and his refusal to take advantage of his friends' ability to provide an escape from death row. Plato thinks he died a hero in defense of his principles; Xenophon, on the other hand, thinks he deliberately manipulated a majority of the jury so that he would not have to face the inevitable disintegration of old age.

Zeno (335–262). Born on the island of Cyprus, Zeno came to Athens around 315 and, after studying with various philosophers, founded the school that gave rise to Stoicism, the most powerful philosophical movement of ancient Greece and Rome. As his family were Phoenicians from the Middle East who had settled in Cyprus, there is good reason for thinking that he was influenced by the Semitic idea that a deity created and still governed the world. Zeno and the Stoics certainly taught that providential reason governs all nature, and that living a good life is thus living "according to nature." He, as well as a number of other Stoics, ended his life by suicide, believing that it was reasonable to assist death when the natural processes of old age and disease announce its coming. The Athenians honored him greatly in life as well as in death. Unfortunately, only fragments of his books survive.

Bibliographical Essay

Probably all authors of introductory books hope that a few readers will be encouraged to study more profoundly the issues touched upon in the text. It is for these readers that a bibliographical essay is included. Here, I touch on technical problems of translation and on some of the major debates swirling around questions of interpretation.

Introduction

Readers not familiar with the controversies within moral philosophy during the past few centuries will find the relevant chapters in Robert Cavalier, James Gouinlock, and James Sterba, eds., *Ethics in the History of Western Philosophy* (New York, 1989) and Lawrence Becker and Charlotte Becker, eds., *A History of Western Ethics* (New York, 1992) helpful starting points. The shift from moralities of obedience based on either divine law or natural law to moralities of autonomy advocating self-governance is ably traced by J. B. Schneewind in *The Invention of Autonomy* (Cambridge, 1998). John Rawls also traces the transition from moralities resting on divine law and natural law to moralities resting on human reasoning and human feeling in his *Lectures on the History of Moral Philosophy* (Cambridge, MA, 2000).

Recent moral philosophy has been dominated by two families of normative theories, one focusing on actions people perform and the other on the expected outcome of actions. Those focusing on actions are called deontological theories and those focusing on outcomes are called consequentialist or utilitarian theories. The classical source of contemporary deontological theories is Immanuel Kant (1724–1804); his seminal works on ethics include *Groundwork of the Metaphysics of Morals* (1785; New York, 1964), *Critique of Practical Reason* (1788; New York, 1956), and most especially *Metaphysics of Morals* (1797; Indianapolis, 1999 [first pt.] and 1983 [second pt.]). For some major developments of Kantian deontological theory, see W. D. Ross, *The Right and the Good* (Indianapolis, [1930] 1988); John Rawls, *A Theory of Justice* (Cambridge, MA, 1971); Thomas Nagel, *The Possibility of Altruism* (Oxford, 1970); Alan Donagan, *The Theory of Morality* (Chicago, 1979); and Jurgen Habermas, *Moral Consciousness and Communicative Action* (Cambridge, MA, 1990).

The classical source of utilitarianism is John Stuart Mill's *Utilitarianism* (1863; Buffalo, 1987), although its roots extend back to Jeremy Bentham's *An Introduction to the Principles of Morals and Legislation* (1789; Amherst, 1988). Major developments in utilitarianism include Richard Brandt, *A Theory of the Good and the Right* (Oxford, 1979); R. M. Hare, *Moral Thinking: Its Levels, Method, and Point* (Oxford, 1981); Derek Parfit, *Reasons and Persons* (Oxford, 1984); and Peter Singer, *Practical Ethics* (Cambridge, 1979).

For an example of care-based ethics, see Nel Noddings, *Caring: A Feminine Approach to Ethics and Moral Education* (Berkeley, 1984). A major book in the revival of casuistry is Albert Jonsen and Stephen Toulmin, *The Abuse of Casuistry: A History of Moral Reasoning* (Berkeley, 1988). For an expressivist or projectivist way of understanding moral thinking see Simon Blackburn, *Ruling Passions: A Theory of Practical Reasoning* (Oxford, 1998).

A seminal article arguing that modern moral philosophy is in a state of confusion and disarray is G. E. M. Anscombe's "Modern Moral Philosophy" (*Philosophy* 33 [1958]). It was reprinted in volume 3 of Anscombe's *Collected Philosophical Papers* (Minneapolis, 1981) and in Roger Crisp and Michael Slote, eds., *Virtue Ethics.* (Oxford, 1997). Another seminal article is Michael Stocker's "The Schizophrenia of Modern Ethical Theories" (*Journal of Philosophy* 73 [1976]), also republished in Crisp and Slote, eds., *Virtue Ethics.* The disarray in modern moral philosophy is famously noted by Alasdair MacIntyre in *After Virtue,* 2d ed. (South Bend, IN, 1983), by Jeffrey Stout in *Ethics after Babel* (Boston, 1988), and by Bernard Williams in *Ethics and the Limits of Philosophy* (Cambridge, MA, 1985). For a scathing critique of modern moral philosophy from outside the field, see Richard Posner, *The Problematics of Moral and Legal Theory*, chaps. 1–2 (Cambridge, MA, 1999). Posner is the Chief Judge of the United States Court of Appeals, Seventh Circuit.

An excellent study showing that ancient Greek ethical theories do not assume that morality is about the central concerns of modern deontological and utilitarian ethical theories—moral obligations, duties, laws, principles, rules, and rights—is Julia Annas, *The Morality of Happiness* (Oxford, 1993). As the title indicates, the Greeks understood ethics not in terms of obeying demands coming from God, nature, others, or even ourselves but in terms of our fulfilling our desire for happiness.

Most readers beginning their study of Greek ethics are faced with an almost insurmountable burden: the inability to read ancient Greek. The burden is even greater for many students because some instructors themselves have never studied Greek. Translations do exist, of course, but translations are confusing because there are no exact English equivalents for many Greek philosophical terms. It is inevitable, then, that different commentators will use different English words for the same key terms in Greek, an unfortunate pitfall for the beginner trying to master technical terms in a philosophical vocabulary.

Fortunately, some translators and authors simply transliterate key terms in their texts—the Greek words appear transcribed into the English alphabet. Thus words such as *psyche* (soul), *phronesis* (prudence), *sophia* (wisdom), *eudaimonia* (happiness), *arete (excellence, virtue), logos* (speech expressing thought, reason), *agathos/kakos* (good/bad), *philia* (love, friendship), *sophrosyne* (temperance), *andreia* (courage), and *dikaisyne* (justice) are often left untranslated in books and articles about Greek ethics. This approach is helpful because it allows the person without Greek to have some idea of the original terms and not be baffled by different English words in various translations and commentaries.

A serious reader will find it worthwhile to take a little time to learn the Greek alphabet and then use a text with the English on one page and the Greek on a facing page, thus seeing first hand how different translators are translating the key terms. The well-known Loeb Classical Library translations, published by Harvard University Press, are helpful in this regard. And a good source of texts and translations from Epicureanism and Stoicism is A. A. Long and D. N. Sedley, *The Hellenistic Philosophers* (Cambridge, 1987). Also valuable is Brad Inwood and Lloyd Gerson, eds., *Hellenistic Philosophy: Introductory Readings*, 2d ed. (Indianapolis, 1998). Unfortunately, our knowledge of Stoicism depends on fragments and on several ancient commentaries, most notably Book III of Cicero's *On Ends* (*De Finibus Bonorum et Malorum*) and Arius Didymus's *Epitome*, both written in the first century B.C.E., and Diogenes Laertius's *Lives of Eminent Philosophers*, Book VII, probably written in the second century B.C.E. The section on Stoic ethics in the *Epitome* appears in English translation in Inwood and Gerson, *Hellenistic Philosophy*. Readers will find some help in F. E. Peters, *Greek Philosophical Terms: A Historical Lexicon* (New York, 1967).

Obviously, most readers will not have the time or the interest to track down the Greek texts and wrestle with problems of just how to understand what the authors were saying; however, it is important, even in an introductory text such as this one, to note that these texts exist and that they are the subject of intense study and debate by experts in ancient philosophy. One goal of this introductory book is to stimulate readers to go back to the original texts, at least in translations accompanied by good commentaries. Learning about the philosophers by reading commentaries is not enough; we need to read the texts themselves. A good place to begin is by studying the first books devoted to ethics ever written and here Terence Irwin's translation with notes of the *Nicomachean Ethics*, 2d ed. (Indianapolis, 1999), Christopher Rowe's translation with an extensive philosophical introduction and commentary by Sarah Broadie (New York, 2002), and Michael Woods's translation with commentary of Books I, II, and VIII of the *Eudemian Ethics*, 2d ed. (Oxford, 1992) are indispensable. Also helpful for those reading Aristotle for the first time is the "philosophy guidebook" by Gerard Hughes, *Aristotle on Ethics* (New York, 2001).

It is not possible to explore the historical and cultural background that influenced the major Greek ethicists in the fourth and third centuries B.C.E. in this introductory book, but awareness of this background is important for understanding how the philosophers were influenced as they generated their ideas. Starting points for reading in this area include Sarah Pomeroy et al., *Ancient Greece: A Political, Social, and Cultural History* (Oxford, 1998) and John Boardman et al., eds., *Greece and the Hellenistic World* (Oxford, 1988). Other reliable but somewhat dated sources for background include two books by A. W. H. Adkins: *Merit and Responsibility: A Study in Greek Values* (Oxford, 1960) and *Moral Values and Political Behavior in Ancient Greece* (New York, 1972). Also of interest is K. J. Dover, *Greek Popular Morality in the Time of Plato and Aristotle* (Oxford, 1974); Walter Burkert, *Greek Religion*, trans. John Raffan (Cambridge, MA, 1985); and E. R. Dodds, *The Greeks and the Irrational* (Berkeley, 1951).

Chapter 1

No writings attributed to Socrates survive, which makes it quite a challenge to distinguish his thinking from that of Plato, who made him a central character in his dialogues. This is the famous "Socratic problem" encountered by scholars trying to sort out when in Plato's works Socrates is speaking as Socrates and when he is merely a mouthpiece for Plato's ideas. The problem is probably insoluble, yet some distinction can be made. Aristotle certainly distinguished what Socrates actually said from what Plato has him say in some later dialogues and so we do the same, following the general line taken by Gregory Vlastos in *Socrates, Ironist and Moral Philosopher*, chap. 2 (Ithaca, NY, 1991) and Terence Irwin in *Plato's Ethics*, chap. 1 (New York, 1995). In general, most scholars believe that Socrates is speaking for himself in the early dialogues but expressing Plato's thoughts in the later ones.

The main textual source for Plato's psychology of desire is Book IV of the *Republic* and also the *Philebus*. For some background on his psychology of desire see Irwin, *Plato's Ethics*, chap. 13; John Cooper, "Plato's Theory of Human Motivations" and "The Psychology of Justice in Plato," both reprinted in Cooper, *Reason and Emotion: Essays on Ancient Moral Psychology and Ethical Theory* (Princeton, NJ, 1999); and Charles Kahn, "Plato's Theory of Desire" in *Review of Metaphysics* 41 (1987). The main textual sources for Aristotle's treatment of desire are Book II of the *Eudemian Ethics*, Book I of *Magna Moralia*, Book II of *De Anima* (*On the Soul*), and Book VII of *Politics*. For further reading, see Jonathan Lear, *Aristotle and the Desire to Understand*, chap. 5 (Cambridge, 1980); Irwin, *Aristotle's First Principles*, chap. 15 (Oxford, 1988); and Cooper, "Some Remarks on Aristotle's Moral Psychology" in his *Reason and Emotion*. For Epicurus's psychology, see Cooper, "Pleasure and Desire in Epicurus" in his *Reason and Emotion*. For the Stoic concept of desire or impulse, see Brad Inwood, *Ethics and Human Action in Early Stoicism*, chap. 4 (Oxford, 1985). Also helpful are the texts and notes in Long and Sedley, *The Hellenistic Philosophers*, sec. 57.

Philippa Foot has provided one of the best responses to the allegations that virtue ethics commits the "naturalistic fallacy" (the effort to derive moral obligations—what we ought to do—from what happens to exist naturally) and relies on an outmoded conception of teleology (the idea that human life is subject to some transcendent preordained goal or finality) in *Natural Goodness* (Oxford, 2001). Also helpful is Michael Thompson's "The Representation of Life" in Rosalind Hursthouse, Gavin Lawrence, and Warren Quinn, *Virtues and Reasons* (Oxford, 1995).

The idea that a legitimate form of self-interest—the desire for personal happiness—is an integral part of virtue ethics is often the target of criticism by ethicists who think our actions should be motivated by duty or by altruism. A good place to begin exploring these issues is the articles in Ellen Paul, Fred Miller, and Jeffrey Paul, eds. *Self-Interest* (Cambridge, 1997). Two articles in *Social Philosophy & Policy* 16 (1999), one by Thomas Hurka titled "The Three Faces of Flourishing" and one by Lester Hunt titled "Flourishing Egoism" are also worthwhile. See also John Cottingham, "The Ethics of Self-Concern," in *Ethics* 101 (1991) and "Partiality and the Virtues" in Roger Crisp, ed., *How Should One Live* (Oxford, 1998), and Douglas Den Uyl, "Teleology and Agent-Centeredness" in *Monist* 65 (1992). As Terence Irwin puts it:

> Plato and Aristotle, therefore, seem to make prudence prior to morality, in the sense that an acceptable defense of the reasonableness of morality must ultimately appeal to prudential considerations, referring to the agent's own interest. ("Prudence and Morality in Greek Ethics." *Ethics* 105 [1995]: 285)

For comments on a highest good or a best good in ancient ethics, what Plato called the *tou agathou idea* (Idea of the good) in Book VI of the *Republic,* and what Aristotle called *ta ariston* (the best) and *to panton akrotaton ton prakton agathon* (the highest of all the goods pursued in actions) in Book I of the *Nicomachean Ethics,* and which came to be known in later moral philosophy as the *"summum bonum"* (highest good), see Hans-Georg Gadamer, *The Idea of the Good in Platonic-Aristotelian Philosophy* (New Haven, CT, 1986); Irwin, *Plato's Ethics,* secs. 186–87; Iris Murdoch, *The Sovereignty of Good* (Boston, 1970) and "The Sovereignty of Good over Other Concepts" in Crisp and Slote, eds., *Virtue Ethics* ; Sarah Broadie, "Aristotle's Elusive *Summum Bonum*" in *Social Philosophy & Policy* 16 (1999); and Richard Kraut, *Aristotle on the Human Good* (Princeton, NJ, 1989) and "Aristotle on the Human Good: An Overview" in Nancy Sherman, ed., *Aristotle's Ethics: Critical Essays* (Lanham, MD, 1999). And, as noted in the text, *Cicero's De Finibus Bonorum et Malorum* is valuable for insights into the positions of Epicurus and the early Stoics on what Cicero called the *summum bonum.*

Chapter 2

Plato's *Euthydemus* offers the best introduction to Socrates' notion of happiness. Plato's own views emerge in the *Gorgias* and the *Republic,* as well as in scattered references in later dialogues. For further reading on happiness in Socrates and Plato see Gregory Vlastos, "Happiness and Virtue in Socrates' Moral Theory" in his *Socrates: Ironist and Moral Philosopher,* as well as his epilogue titled "Felix Socrates." See also numerous references in Irwin, *Plato's Ethics,* as well as Irwin's "Socrates the Epicurean" in Hugh Benson, ed., *Essays on the Philosophy of Socrates* (New York, 1992).

Annas's *The Morality of Happiness* is an indispensable source for ancient philosophical views on happiness, especially the views of Aristotle, the Stoics, and Epicurus. Also see Annas's article "Virtue and Eudaimonism" in Paul, Miller, and Paul, eds., *Virtue and Vice.*

The major sources for Aristotle's conception of happiness are Books I and X of the *Nicomachean Ethics* and Book II of the *Eudemian Ethics*. For examples of the extensive literature on Aristotle's views, see Anthony Kenny, *Aristotle on the Perfect Life* (Oxford, 1992); and Thomas Nagel, "Aristotle on *Eudaimonia*," J. L. Ackrill, "Aristotle on *Eudaimonia*," and John McDowell, "The Role of *Eudaimonia* in Aristotle's Ethics," all in Amélie Oksenberg Rorty, ed., *Essays on Aristotle's Ethics* (Berkeley, 1980). Carlo Natali, *The Wisdom of Aristotle* (Albany, 2001), chap. 4, provides a clear summary of Aristotle's views. Chap. 6 of Foot's *Natural Goodness*, titled "Happiness and Human Good," is also excellent. Terence Irwin discusses the lasting quality of happiness in "Permanent Happiness: Aristotle and Solon" in Nancy Sherman, ed., *Aristotle's Ethics*. See also chaps. 16–17 in Irwin's *Aristotle's First Principles* (Oxford, 1990); and chap. 1 in Jonathan Lear, *Happiness, Death, and the Remainder of Life* (Cambridge, MA, 2000). Lear's book is a provocative discussion of Aristotle's concept of happiness from the perspective of Freud and psychoanalysis.

Also important is Stephen White, *Sovereign Virtue: Aristotle on the Relation between Happiness and Prosperity* (Stanford, 1992) and Cooper, "Contemplation and Happiness," in his *Reason and Emotion*. A very perceptive article is Robert Heinaman, "Rationality, *Eudaimonia*, and *Kakodaimonia* in Aristotle," *Phronesis* 38 (1993). *Kakodaimonia* means unhappiness or a wretched fate. Heinaman shows that virtuous behavior is not always behavior for the sake of happiness; sometimes virtue cannot promote happiness because the person is trapped in a tragic situation where happiness is no longer a possibility. In such circumstances all the person can do is choose the lesser evil. An earlier article by Heinaman, "*Eudaimonia* and Self-Sufficiency in the *Nicomachean Ethics*," *Phronesis* 33 (1988), is also worthwhile.

Two articles in Malcolm Schofield and Gisela Striker, eds., *The Norms of Nature* (Cambridge, 1986) are helpful for understanding the Epicurean and Stoic conceptions of happiness: Malte Hossenfelder, "Epicurus—Hedonist *malgré lui*" and Terence Irwin, "Stoic and Aristotelian Conceptions of Happiness." See also A. A. Long, "Stoic eudaimonism," chap. 8 in his *Stoic Studies* (Cambridge, 1996), and Cooper, "Eudaimonism, the Appeal to Nature, and 'Moral Duty' in Stoicism," in his *Reason and Emotion*.

Chapter 3

For summaries of prephilosophical ideas of virtue see A. W. H. Adkins, *Moral Values and Political Behavior in Ancient Greece* and *Merit and Responsibility: A Study in Greek Values* (New York, 1972). His article, "Plato," in Cavalier, Gouinlock, and Sterba, eds., *Ethics in the History of Western Philosophy,* provides a more succinct summary of the ideas about virtue that were prevalent when Socrates and Plato began to rethink the topic. K. J. Dover's *Greek Popular Morality at the Time of Plato and Aristotle* and chaps. 6 and 7 of E. R. Dodds's classic *The Greeks and the Irrational* are also helpful. Terence Irwin shows how the philosophers modified the prephilosophical notions of virtue in "The Virtues: Theory and Common Sense in Greek Philosophy," which appears in Crisp, ed., *How Should One Live?*

For the distinction between the character virtues (*aretai ethikai*) and the intellectual virtues (*aretai dianoetikai*) in Aristotle, see the *Nicomachean Ethics,* Book I, chap. 13 and Book VI, chap. 1, and the *Eudemian Ethics,* Book II, chap. 1. W. W. Fortenbaugh explores this distinction in "Aristotle's Distinction between Moral Virtue and Practical Wisdom" in John Anton and Anthony Preus, eds., *Aristotle's Ethics* (Albany, 1991). For a thoughtful criticism of Aristotle's distinction between the intellectual and the moral virtues, see Linda Trinkaus Zagzebski, *Virtues of the Mind: An Inquiry into the Nature of Virtue and the Ethical Foundations of Knowledge* (Cambridge, 1996).

Aristotle's important distinction between *natural* character virtue, which originates in our natural dispositions to be courageous, fair, generous, and so forth, and *authentic* or "*full*" character virtue, which is acquired by our deliberate choices, is found in the *Nicomachean Ethics,* Book VI, chap. 13. The crucial distinction between natural and authentic character virtue is not well emphasized in the contemporary literature but see Irwin's remarks at p. 254 of his translation of the *Nicomachean Ethics.* Carlo Natali also notes the distinction in his *The Wisdom of Aristotle,* pp. 150–54, as does Stephen White, *Sovereign Virtue,* pp. 100–108, and Richard Kraut, *Aristotle and the Human Good,* pp. 247–51.

For the distinction between goods or good things and the authentic virtues in Aristotle, see Cooper, "Aristotle and the Goods of Fortune" in *Reason and Emotion*; White, *Sovereign Virtue*, chap. 2; and Anthony Kenny, *Aristotle on the Perfect Life*.

For the translation of the word *hexis* as "state" rather than "habit" or "disposition" see Terence Irwin's translation of the *Nicomachean Ethics* and his remarks on pp. 196 and 349. Michael Woods also translates *hexis* as "state" in his translation of Books I, II, and VIII of the *Eudemian Ethics*. See also J. O. Urmson, *Aristotle's Ethics* (Oxford, 1988), chap. 2; Martha Nussbaum, *The Fragility of Goodness* (Cambridge, 1986), p. 494 n.11; Jonathan Lear, *Aristotle: The Desire to Understand*, pp. 164–74; and Nancy Sherman, *The Fabric of Character: Aristotle's Theory of Virtue* (Oxford, 1989), chap. 5; and Sherman, "The Habituation of Character" in her *Aristotle's Ethics*. Stephen Salkever makes a good case for translating *hexis* as "state" in *Finding the Mean* (Princeton, NJ, 1990), pp. 78–80. Similarly, Julia Annas acknowledges that "state" is the "established translation" in her discussion of *hexis* in *The Morality of Happiness*, pp. 48–52. Examples of other translations of *hexis* are "habitual disposition" (Hughes, *Aristotle on Ethics*, p. 54f.), and "fixed disposition or character" (Aristide Tessitore, *Reading Aristotle's Ethics* [Albany, 1996], p. 25).

The word *philia* poses a tremendous problem for translators. It designates various personal relationships that we would sometimes describe as love, sometimes as friendship, and sometimes as mere friendliness. Aristotle says that the range of possible *philia* is as extensive as the range of justice—the relationship of *philia* can occur with any one with whom we have contacts. The *Nicomachean Ethics* acknowledges that the word *philia* can describe relationships between romantic lovers (NE 1156b2), among colleagues (NE 1158a28), among people traveling together or among soldiers (NE 1159b28), among members of the same religious group or dinner club (NE 1160a19), among members of the same tribe (NE 1161b14), and between vendors and those buying from them (NE 1163b35). It also describes the relationship between two virtuous people devoted to pursuing the good of the other for the sake of the other—a relationship Aristotle calls an authentic or perfect *philia*, as well as the relationships between husband and wife, and between parents and their children. Depending on the context, then, *philia* will mean love, friendship, or friendliness, with love being the best translation for relationships of *philia* based on virtue, marriage, or family ties. It is not without interest to note that Aristotle apparently had a good marriage with Pythias, the mother of his daughter, and then, after she died, a close relationship with Herpyllis, the mother of his son Nicomachus.

Is love (*philia*) a character virtue for Aristotle? According to some commentators, Anthony Kenny, for example (*Aristotle on the Perfect Life*, p. 43), love and friendship (*philia*) in Aristotle is a great good but cannot be one of the virtues because it is a relationship involving at least two people rather than a character state of one person. Yet Aristotle does not think that the relationship aspect of *philia* rules out its being a virtue. *Philia*, he says, "is a virtue or involves virtue" (NE 1155a1). This is an ambiguous phrase; it could indicate he is unsure whether *philia* is a virtue or it could indicate that *philia* is a virtue in some cases and a good that involves virtue in other cases. However, in other texts Aristotle explicitly designates *philia* as one of the character virtues. He includes it in his enumeration of virtues in the *Nichomachean Ethics* (NE 1108a26–30) and in his famous table of virtues in the *Eudemian Ethics* (EE 1220b36–1221a12). Aristotle clearly makes *philia* more than an external good when he lists it as a virtue. Aristotle does say that *friends* are external goods; in fact, they are the greatest of external goods (NE 1169b10). However, saying that *friends* are external goods is not the same as saying that *friendship* or *love* is an external good. Friends and lovers can be external goods while *engaging* in friendship and love is a virtuous activity that forms one's character.

Liddell and Scott's *Greek-English Lexicon* (New York, 1985), pp. 1933–34, gives "affectionate regard" and "friendship" as the primary meanings of the noun *philia*. It also gives "to love" as the primary meaning of *philein*, the verb from which the noun *philia* is derived, and it lists its antonym as *misein* which means "to hate." Most scholars readily translate the verb *philein* as "to love" in appropriate contexts—Nussbaum, *The Fragility of Goodness*, p. 354; Stephen White, *Sovereign Virtue*, pp. 294ff.; and Terence Irwin in his translations of the *Nicomachean Ethics* and other works, for example.

Yet some scholars do insist that "to love" is not an appropriate translation for *philein*. Cooper, in "Friendship and the Good in Aristotle," in his *Reason and Emotion*, says much harm is caused by translators who render *philein* as "to love." Cooper prefers to translate *philein* as "to like" and he reserves "to love" for the Greek verb *stergein*. But Aristotle uses *stergein*, no less than *philein*, in a wide range of applications. *Stergein* denotes, for example, the love a craftsman has for his work (NE 1168a7) as well as the love of a person for his dear friend.

Moreover, translating *philein* as "to like" instead of "to love" makes it difficult to discuss Aristotle's concern with the question of whether one ought to love himself more than anyone else. The question loses much of its impact if *philein* in this context is translated as "liking yourself" more than "liking anyone else" (NE 1163a28, 1163b10), and if *philautos* (NE 1168a29–1169b1) is translated as "self-liker" or "liker of self" instead of the familiar "self-lover" or "lover of self."

In fact, Aristotle tells us that we praise people for loving their friends, thus recognizing that "loving (*philein*) is the *virtue* (*arete*) of friends" (NE 1159a35). Love (*philein*) builds the relationship (*philia*), and enduring love builds enduring relationships (NE 1159a36). Depending on the context, then, a good case can be made for translating *philia* sometimes as "love," sometimes as "friendship," and sometimes as "friendliness"; and for making love (as well as friendship) count as one of the character virtues alongside justice, courage, temperance, and so forth.

For background reading on *megalopsychia*, which we are translating as "pride," see Tara Smith, "The Practice of Pride" in Paul, Miller, and Paul, eds. *Virtue and Vice* (1998); W. F. R. Hardie, "Magnanimity in Aristotle's Ethics," *Phronesis* 23 (1978); and Tessitore, *Reading Aristotle's Ethics: Virtue, Rhetoric, and Political Philosophy*, pp. 28–35.

For the view that all the major Greek philosophers agreed that having "any one of the virtues, where the term *virtue* is carefully and strictly applied, means that you have to have all the rest as well," see Cooper "The Unity of Virtue," in his *Reason and Emotion*. See also, Annas, *The Morality of Happiness*, pp. 73–84; Irwin, "The Virtues: Theory and Common Sense in Greek Philosophy," in Crisp, ed., *How Should One Live*. Plato depicted Socrates in the *Protagoras* arguing that the virtues must be a unity because they are all aspects of wisdom. Later, in Book IV of the *Republic*, Plato argues that there are other virtues besides wisdom but that they are all inseparable. However, in the late dialogue the *Statesman* Plato depicts the speaker known as the Stranger, who seems to speak for Plato, arguing that virtues can conflict, the same position that Socrates had rejected in the *Protagoras* and in the *Republic*. Does this represent a change in Plato's position? Perhaps, but the arguments in the *Statesman* are notoriously weak, and Plato seems to be talking about natural virtue and its tendencies to pull us in different directions rather than authentic virtue, which is the result of reasoning. See Irwin, *Plato's Ethics*, chap. 20; and Cooper, "The Unity of Virtue," in his *Reason and Emotion.* For Socrates' original position see Terry Penner, "The Unity of Virtue," in Hugh Benson, ed., *Essays on the Philosophy of Socrates* (1992) and Gregory Vlastos, "The Unity of the Virtues in the *Protagoras*," in his *Platonic Studies,* 2d ed. (Princeton, NJ, 1981). The unity of the authentic or full moral virtues in Aristotle is clear: they all depend on the single intellectual virtue of *phronesis* (NE 1145a1–2), which creates them by repeatedly choosing the actions that form them in our character. And the unity of the virtues is also seen in Zeno, who seems to have held that temperance, courage, and justice are merely names for prudence in different areas of life. See the texts and discussion in Long and Sedley, *The Hellenistic Philosophers*, sec. 61.

Chapter 4

John Cottingham provides a good summary of the central role of reason in the works of Plato, Aristotle, Epicurus, and the Stoics in his *Philosophy and the Good Life*, chap. 2. For Socrates' well-known view that virtue is knowledge or wisdom, see Irwin, *Plato's Ethics*, esp. secs. 38–44, 79–82, 96–103; and chap. 3 in Irwin, *Plato's Moral Theory: The Early and Middle Dialogues* (Oxford, 1977); Gerasimos Santas, "Socrates at Work on Virtue and Knowledge," in Gregory Vlastos, ed., *The Philosophy of Socrates: A Collection of Critical Essays* (New York, 1971); and Alexander Nehamas, "Socratic Intellectualism," in John Cleary, ed., *Proceedings of the Boston Area Colloquium in Ancient Philosophy*, vol. 2 (Lanham, MD, 1987). An extended discussion by Martha

Nussbaum of Socrates' views on practical reasoning in the *Protagoras* can be found in chap. 4 of *The Fragility of Goodness*. Chaps. 12–17 in Irwin's *Plato's Ethics* explore the role of knowledge and practical reason in the *Republic;* chap. 19 discuses the special role of practical intelligence and prudence (*nous* and *phronesis*) in managing pleasures as elaborated in the *Philebus*, and chap. 20 gives an account of the changing role of *phronesis* in the *Statesman* and the *Laws*. See also George Klosko, "The Rule of Reason in Plato's Psychology," *History of Philosophy Quarterly* 5 (1988). For more on Plato's emphasis in his late works on educating people to become virtuous by exercising their own reasoning rather than by simply following the philosopher-kings, the approach favored in the *Republic*, see Cooper, "Plato's *Statesman* and Politics," in his *Reason and Emotion*.

The word "*phronesis*" appears in almost all of Plato's dialogues, most frequently in the *Laws* (twenty-seven times), the *Republic* (eighteen times), the *Phaedo* (fifteen times), and the *Meno* (fourteen times), and the meaning of the word varies with its context, ranging from theoretical knowledge to practical knowledge useful for guiding the choices we make in life. Unfortunately the most comprehensive study of *phronesis* in Plato, H. J. Schaeffer's *"Phronesis" bei Platon* (Bochum, 1981), has not been translated. Schaeffer shows how the term evolved through many uses. To the best of my knowledge, there is no extended analysis of *phronesis* in Plato in English. An article in French is helpful: Monique Dixsaut, "De quoi les philosophes sont-ils amoureux? Note sur la *phronèsis* dans les dialogues de Platon," in Chateau, ed., *La Vérité Pratique* (Paris, 1997).

Chapter 5

The literature on prudence in Aristotle is so extensive that only a sampling can be mentioned here. One of the best introductions is Norman Dahl, *Practical Reason, Aristotle, and Weakness of the Will* (Minneapolis, 1984), chaps. 1–8 and App. I. Three other excellent starting points in books are the summaries by Gadamer in *Truth and Method,* 2d ed. (New York, 1991), pp. 312–24; Joseph Dunne,

Back to the Rough Ground: "Phronesis" and "Techne" in Modern Philosophy and in Aristotle (Notre Dame, IN, 1993), chaps. 8–9; and Nussbaum, *The Fragility of Goodness*, chap. 10. Nussbaum expanded on this chapter in "The Discernment of Perception: An Aristotelian Conception of Private and Public Rationality" in Sherman, ed., *Aristotle's Ethics.*

The *Rhetoric* is not a work devoted to ethical theory; therefore, the remarks about *phronesis* and the character virtues are not as substantive as the treatments in the *Nicomachean Ethics* and the *Politics.* Nonetheless, they are of interest and philosophers are attentive to the relation of the *Rhetoric* with Aristotle's ethical works. See, for example, Terence Irwin, "Ethics in the *Rhetoric* and in the Ethics"; Troels Engbert-Pedersen, "Is There an Ethical Dimension to Aristotelian Rhetoric?"; Stephen Halliwell, "The Challenge of Rhetoric to Political and Ethical Theory in Aristotle"; all in Amélie Oksenberg Rorty, *Essays on Aristotle's Rhetoric* (Berkeley, 1996). Halliwell's article is an abbreviated and modified version of his "Popular Morality, Philosophical Ethics, and the *Rhetoric*," which appeared in David Furley and Alexander Nehamas, eds., *Aristotle's Rhetoric: Philosophical Essays* (Princeton, NJ, 1994). Of interest also is Cooper's "Ethical-Political Theory in Aristotle's *Rhetoric*," in his *Reason and Emotion.* For a discussion of *phronesis* and its relations to character virtue and feeling in the *Rhetoric,* see Eugene Garver, *Aristotle's Rhetoric: An Art of Character* (Chicago, 1994), chaps. 4–6 and 8.

Some representative examples of commentaries and interpretations of *phronesis* in the ethical works are Carlo Natali, *The Wisdom of Aristotle*, chaps. 1–2; Gerard Hughes, *Aristotle on Ethics*, chap. 5; Troels Engberg-Pedersen, *Aristotle's Theory of Moral Insight* (Oxford, 1983), chaps. 6–9; C. D. C. Reeve, *Practices of Reason: Aristotle's Nicomachean Ethics* (Oxford, 1995), chap. 2; Charles Larmore, *Patterns of Moral Complexity* (Cambridge, 1987), chap. 1; Douglas Den Uyl, *The Virtue of Prudence* (New York, 1991), chap. 1; and Foot, *Natural Goodness*, chap. 4. Also of interest on this topic is Zagzebski, *Virtues of the Mind*, pp. 211–31. Zagzebski argues that the virtue of *phronesis* is "a higher-order virtue that governs the entire range of moral and intellectual virtues" (p. 229).

Among other important articles are Richard Sorabji's "Aristotle on the Role of Intellect in Virtue" and David Wiggins's "Deliberation and Practical Reason," both in Rorty, ed., *Essays on Aristotle's Ethics*. Also of major importance are Deborah Modrak's "Aristotle on Reason, Practical Reason, and Living Well," in Anton and Preus, eds., *Aristotle's Ethics*; Beatriz Bossi de Kirchner, "On the Power of Practical Reason" in the *Review of Metaphysics* 43 (1989); and D. P. Dryer, "Aristotle's Conception of *Orthos Logos*," *Monist* 66 (1983). "*Orthos logos*" means "right reason" and the "right reason" for ethical decision making is *phronesis* according to Aristotle (NE 1144b27–28).

The most extensive relatively recent commentary (1958–1959; Louvain, 1970 [2d ed.]) on the *Nicomachean Ethics* is René Gauthier and Jean Jolif's two volume *L'Ethique a Nicomaque*. Gauthier and Jolif, however, make two questionable moves in their work. First, they translate "*orthos logos*," as "la droite règle" or "the right rule," which gives the impression that Aristotle was proposing a rule-based ethic. Second, in their commentary, they claim that Aristotle made *duty* the center of his ethics ("Aristote a mis au centre même de sa morale l'idée distincte de 'devoir' moral," 2:571), thus giving the impression that Aristotle proposed a duty-based ethics.

There is a long-standing debate, dating to the nineteenth century, over the role Aristotle gave *phronesis* in his virtue theory that is relevant to the approach taken in this chapter. Some authors, following a remark by Aristotle that character virtue sets the ends and prudence figures out the means (NE 1145a4–6), view the character virtues as setting the goals that direct our lives. Thus the intellectual virtue of prudence should not be given the leading role in the development of a good life because its role is merely instrumental—it can only show us how to achieve a goal set by character virtue. It is the character virtues—justice, courage, temperance, and so forth—that determine what is good, not prudence.

See, for example, W. W. Fortenbaugh, *Aristotle on Emotions* (London, 1975) and "Aristotle's Distinction between Moral Virtue and Practical Wisdom," in Anton and Preus, eds., *Aristotle's Ethics*; Carlo Natali, *The Wisdom of Aristotle*, chap. 2; Alasdair MacIntyre, *Whose Justice? Whose Rationality?* (Notre Dame, IN, 1988), chap. 8; Pierre Aubenque, *La Prudence chez Aristote*, 3d ed. (Paris, 1986), chap. 3; Thomas Tuozzo, "Aristotelian Deliberation Is Not of Ends" in Anton and Preus, eds. *Aristotle's Ethics*; and A. D. Smith, "Character and Intellect in Aristotle's Ethics," *Phronesis* 41 (1995).

The approach taken in this book follows instead the general interpretation suggested by other commentators who give prudence the crucial role in determining what we should do. See, for example, the work of John Cooper, Terence Irwin, Norman Dahl, Troels Engberg-Pedersen, Gerald Hughes, C. D. C. Reeve, John Cottingham, Rosalind Hursthouse, Nancy Sherman, Martha Nussbaum, and others, as noted in the citations above. See also Alfred Mele, "Choice and Virtue in the *Nicomachean Ethics,*" *Journal of the History of Philosophy* 19 (1981); and "Aristotle on the Roles of Reason in Motivation and Judgment," *Archiv für Geschichte der Philosophie* 66 (1983); D. P. Dryer, "Aristotle's Conception of *Orthos Logos,*"; and Jean-Yves Chateau, "L'Objet de la *Phronèsis* et la Vérité Pratique" in Chateau, ed., *La Vérité Pratique* (Paris: 1997).

In general, these authors tend to understand *phronesis* as the decisive virtue for ethical decision making. Undoubtedly, in many cases a virtuous person acts with little or no deliberation and prudential reasoning, and this gives the appearance that character virtue and not *phronesis* is moving the *authentically* virtuous person to action. However, for Aristotle, *authentic* character virtue is produced only by repeated choices made "according to right reason." Hence, as was explained in the text, the intellectual virtue of *phronesis* is the ruling virtue: it either actually deliberates here and now to find what is reasonable or it has repeatedly deliberated so well in the past that well-developed *authentic* character virtue now enables the person to respond reasonably in many situations with little or no deliberation. This seems to be the interpretation of Aristotle's greatest medieval commentator, Thomas Aquinas. See, for example, *Summa Theologiae* Ia IIae, q. 57, a. 4–6 and IIa IIae, a. 47–57. Daniel Nelson captures Aquinas's position nicely in his *The Priority of Prudence: Virtue and Natural Law in Thomas Aquinas and the Implications for Modern Ethics* (University Park, PA, 1992).

The debate over whether *phronesis* is about means only and therefore subject to the character virtues, or whether it is about both means and ends, and therefore the character virtues are subject to it, might never be resolved to everyone's satisfaction—each side, as Chateau observes, can find texts of Aristotle supporting its claim. Aristotle makes it clear that both character virtue and prudence are needed for good decision making; unfortunately, his language describing how character virtue and intellectual virtue or prudence are related is sometimes ambiguous.

Chapter 6

As noted previously, we do not have good accounts of early Stoic ethics because none of their complete works survives. Scholars generally rely on three later sources: Cicero's *De Finibus*, which dates from the first century B.C.E.; some excerpts in John Strobaeus, a fourth century writer; and Book VII of Diogenes Laertius's *Lives of Eminent Philosophers*, probably written in the second century. Diogenes summarizes the thought of Zeno at great length, and also comments on several other leading figures— Cleanthes, Ariston, and Chrysippus. The texts and translations of Cicero's *De Finibus* and of Diogenes' *Lives* are available in the Loeb Classical Library series published by Harvard University Press.

Cicero's understanding of the Stoic Panaetius is found in his *De Officiis* and is of some value for understanding Stoic ideas about decision making. Unfortunately the title *"De Officiis"* is sometimes translated into English as *"On Moral Duties"* and this is misleading. Although the word *officium* can mean "duty" in Latin, its primary meaning is a "service," or a "favor," or a "kindness," or a "courtesy" that one performs for someone. Cicero was using the Latin word *"officium"* in his *"De Officiis"* to translate *"Peri Kathekontos,"* which was the title of Panaetius's book, now unfortunately lost. However, *kathekonta* in Panaetius and the other Stoics does not designate anything moral. As we saw in chap. 3, *kathekonta* simply means "appropriate actions" for the Stoics. The "appropriate actions" are not moral actions; the word designating morally virtuous actions in Stoicism is *katorthomata*. The *katorthomata* are appropriate actions performed with a virtuous disposition, and such actions are not really moral *duties*. The phrase *"On Moral Duties,"* then, is a misleading translation of Cicero's *"De Officiis"* and does not do justice to Panaetius's theory of ethical decision making, which is not a duty-based ethics.

What is perhaps the best study of *phronesis* in the Stoics is unfortunately not available in English: Danielle Lories, *Le Sens Commun et le Jugement du "Phronimos:" Aristote et les Stoïciens* (Louvain-la-Neuve, 1998), esp. chap. 6. In chap. 6, Lories demonstrates that the Stoics, who did not sharply distinguish *sophia* and *phronesis* as Aristotle had done, nonetheless preserved the distinctive characteristics of Aristotle's *phronesis* in their discussions of practical reasoning and decision making. And the Stoic *sophos* or sage, no less than the Aristotelian *phronimos*, is thus the person who has achieved excellence in prudential reasoning and determines for oneself the reasonable course of action aimed at achieving a good life in the ever-changing circumstances of a contingent world. According to Lories, the Stoics, no less than Aristotle, made *sophia/phronesis* the intellectual virtue governing the character virtues because it determines in each situation just what response is just or loving, or whether, given the situation, it is not prudent to seek justice or love. Lories argues with considerable cogency that early Stoicism was an ethic of prudence no less than the ethics of Aristotle.

For another view see J. M. Rist, "An Early Dispute about Right Reason," *Monist* 66 (1983). Rist argues that the Stoics moved away from Aristotle's concept of prudence by identifying right reason with the reason of Zeus. Brad Inwood, in *Ethics and Human Action in Early Stoicism*, also represents an alternative to Lories's interpretation when he states that the early Stoics allowed no place for deliberation in the determination of actions, which are governed instead by one set of principles derived from the will of Zeus. "Odd as it may sound," he writes, "this set of principles must have been what the Stoics meant by the virtue of prudence (*phronesis*)" (p. 107). No such oddity appears in Lories's interpretation of the Stoic virtue of *phronesis*.

Finally, for some early fragments on prudence and the other virtues, and brief commentaries, see Long and Sedley, *The Hellenistic Philosophers*, secs. 61, 66. Also helpful is A. C. Lloyd, "Emotion and Decision in Stoic Psychology," in J. Rist, *The Stoics* (Berkeley, 1978).

Bibliography

A number of the works listed here are cited in abbreviated form in the text. The abbreviated citation appears in brackets following the respective title below.

Ackrill, J. L. "Aristotle on *Eudaimonia*." In *Essays on Aristotle's Ethics.* Ed. Amélie Oksenberg Rorty. Berkeley: University of California Press, 1980.

Adkins, A. W. H. "Plato." In *Ethics in the History of Western Philosophy.* Ed. Robert Cavalier, James Gouinlock, and James Sterba. New York: St. Martin's Press, 1989.

———. *Moral Values and Political Behavior in Ancient Greece.* New York: W. W. Norton & Co., 1972.

———. *Merit and Responsibility: A Study in Greek Values.* Oxford: Oxford University Press, 1960.

Annas, Julia. "Virtue and Eudaimonism." In *Virtue and Vice.* Ed. Ellen Paul, Fred Miller, and Jeffrey Paul. Cambridge: Cambridge University Press, 1998.

———. *The Morality of Happiness.* Oxford: Oxford University Press, 1993.

Anscombe, G. E. M. *Collected Philosophical Papers.* Vol. 3. Minneapolis: University of Minnesota Press, 1981.

———. "Modern Moral Philosophy." *Philosophy* 33 (1958): 1–19.

Anton, John, and Anthony Preus, eds. *Aristotle's Ethics.* Albany: State University of New York Press, 1991.

Aquinas, Thomas. *Summa Theologiae.* Latin text and English translation. New York: McGraw-Hill, 1968.

Aristotle. *Nicomachean Ethics.* Trans. Terence Irwin. 2d ed. Indianapolis: Hackett Publishing Company, 1999.

———. *Eudemian Ethics* [EE]. Books I, II, and VIII. Trans. Michael Woods. 2d ed. Oxford: Oxford University Press, 1992.

————. *Politics* [*Pol.*]. Loeb Classical Library. Cambridge, MA: Harvard University Press, 1990.

————. *On the Soul, Parva Naturalia, On Breath*. Loeb Classical Library. Cambridge, MA: Harvard University Press, 1988.

————. *Nichomachean Ethics* [NE]. Loeb Classical Library. Cambridge, MA: Harvard University Press, 1982.

— ————. *Rhetoric* [Rh]. Loeb Classical Library. Cambridge, MA: Harvard University Press, 1982.

————. *Athenian Constitution, Eudemian Ethics, Virtues and Vices*. Loeb Classical Library. Cambridge, MA: Harvard University Press, 1981.

————. *Metaphysics 10–14, Oeconomica, and Magna Moralia*. Loeb Classical Library. Cambridge, MA: Harvard University Press, 1977.

Aubenque, Pierre. *La Prudence chez Aristote*, 3d ed. Paris: Presses Universitaires de France, 1986.

Becker, Lawrence, and Charlotte Becker, eds. *A History of Western Ethics*. New York: Garland Publishing, 1992.

Benson, Hugh, ed. *Essays on the Philosophy of Socrates*. New York: Oxford University Press, 1992.

Bentham, Jeremy. *An Introduction to the Principles of Morals and Legislation*. Amherst, NY: Prometheus Books, 1988.

Blackburn, Simon. *Ruling Passions: A Theory of Practical Reasoning*. Oxford: Oxford University Press, 1998.

Boardman, John, Jasper Griffin, and Oswyn Murray. *Greece and the Hellenistic World*. Oxford: Oxford University Press, 1988.

Bossi de Kirchner, Beatriz. "On the Power of Practical Reason." *Review of Metaphysics* 43 (1989): 47–71

Brandt, Richard. *A Theory of the Good and the Right*. Oxford: Oxford University Press, 1979.

Broadie, Sarah. "Aristotle's Elusive *Summum Bonum.*" *Social Philosophy & Policy* 16 (1999): 233–51.

————. *Ethics with Aristotle*. Oxford: Oxford University Press, 1991.

Burkert, Walter. *Greek Religion*. Trans. John Raffan. Cambridge, MA: Harvard University Press, 1985.

Cavalier, Robert, James Gouinlock, and James Sterba, eds. *Ethics in the History of Western Philosophy*. New York: St. Martin's Press, 1989.

Chateau, Jean-Yves, ed. *La Vérité Pratique*. Paris: Librairie Philosophique J. Vrin, 1997.

————. "L'Objet de la *Phronèsis* et la Vérité Pratique." In *La Vérité Pratique*. Ed. Jean-Yves Chateau. Paris: Librairie Philosophique J. Vrin, 1997.

Cicero. *De Finibus Bonorum et Malorum*. Loeb Classical Library. Cambridge, MA: Harvard University Press, 1983.

———. *De Officiis*. Loeb Classical Library. Cambridge, MA: Harvard University Press, 1975.

Cleary, John, ed. *Proceedings of the Boston Area Colloquium in Ancient Philosophy*. Vol. 2. Lanham, MD: University Press of America, 1987.

Cooper, John. *Reason and Emotion: Essays on Ancient Moral Psychology and Ethical Theory*. Princeton, NJ: Princeton University Press, 1999.

———. *Reason and the Human Good in Aristotle*. Cambridge, MA: Harvard University Press, 1975.

Cottingham, John. *Philosophy and the Good Life*. Cambridge: Cambridge University Press, 1998.

———. "Partiality and the Virtues." In *How Should One Live? Essays on the Virtues*. Ed. Roger Crisp. Oxford: Oxford University Press, 1998.

———. "The Ethics of Self-Concern." *Ethics* 101 (1991): 798–817.

Crisp, Roger, ed. *How Should One Live? Essays on the Virtues*. Oxford: Oxford University Press, 1998.

Crisp, Roger, and Michael Slote, eds. *Virtue Ethics*. Oxford: Oxford University Press, 1997.

Dahl, Norman. *Practical Reason, Aristotle, and Weakness of the Will*. Minneapolis: University of Minnesota Press, 1984.

Den Uyl, Douglas. "Teleology and Agent-Centeredness." *Monist* 65 (1992): 14–33.

———. *The Virtue of Prudence*. New York: Peter Lang, 1991.

Dixsaut, Monique. "De quoi les philosophes sont-ils amoureux? Note sur la *phronèsis* dans les dialogues de Platon." In *La Vérité Pratique*. Ed. Jean-Yves Chateau. Paris: Librairie Philosophique J. Vrin, 1997.

Dodds, E. R. *The Greeks and the Irrational*. Berkeley: University of California Press, 1951.

Donagan, Alan. *The Theory of Morality*. Chicago: University of Chicago Press, 1979.

Dover, K. J. *Greek Popular Morality in the Time of Plato and Aristotle*. Oxford: Oxford University Press, 1974.

Dryer, D. P. "Aristotle's Conception of *Orthos Logos*." *Monist* 66 (1983): 106–19.

Dunne, John. *Back to the Rough Ground: "Phronesis" and "Techne" in Modern Philosophy and in Aristotle*. Notre Dame, IN: University of Notre Dame Press, 1993.

Engbert-Pedersen, Troels. "Is There an Ethical Dimension to Aristotelian Rhetoric?" In *Essays on Aristotle's Rhetoric*. Ed. Amélie Oksenberg Rorty. Berkeley: University of California Press, 1996.

———. *Aristotle's Theory of Moral Insight*. Oxford: Oxford University Press, 1983.

Engstrom, Stephen, and Jennifer Whiting, eds. *Aristotle, Kant, and the Stoics.* Cambridge: Cambridge University Press, 1996.

Foot, Philippa. *Natural Goodness.* Oxford: Oxford University Press, 2001.

Fortenbaugh, W. W. "Aristotle's Distinction between Moral Virtue and Practical Wisdom." In *Aristotle's Ethics.* Ed. John Anton and Anthony Preus. Albany: State University of New York Press, 1991.

———. *Aristotle on Emotions.* London: Gerald Duckworth & Co., 1975.

Furley, David, and Alexander Nehamas, eds. *Aristotle's* Rhetoric*: Philosophical Essays.* Princeton, NJ: Princeton University Press, 1994.

Gadamer, Hans-Georg. *Truth and Method*, 2d ed. Trans. Joel Weinsheimer and Donald Marshall. New York: Crossroad Publishing, 1991.

———. *The Idea of the Good in Platonic-Aristotelian Philosophy.* Trans. P. Christopher Smith. New Haven, CT: Yale University Press, 1986.

Garver, Eugene. *Aristotle's* Rhetoric: *An Art of Character.* Chicago: University of Chicago Press, 1994.

Gauthier, Rene, and Jean Jolif. *L'Ethique à Nicomaque.* Vol. 1: Translation. Vol. 2: Commentary. Louvain: Publications Universitaire de Louvain, 1958–1959; 2d ed., 1970.

Habermas, Jurgen. *Moral Consciousness and Communicative Action.* Trans. Christian Lenhardt and Shierry Weber-Nicholsen. Cambridge, MA: MIT Press, 1990.

Halliwell, Stephen. "The Challenge of Rhetoric to Political and Ethical Theory in Aristotle." In *Essays on Aristotle's* Rhetoric. Ed. Amélie Oksenberg Rorty. Berkeley: University of California Press, 1996.

———. "Popular Morality, Philosophical Ethics, and the *Rhetoric.*" In *Aristotle's* Rhetoric: *Philosophical Essays.* Ed. David Furley and Alexander Nehamas. Princeton, NJ: Princeton University Press, 1994.

Hardie, W. F. R. "Magnanimity in Aristotle's Ethics." *Phronesis* 23 (1978): 63–79.

Hare, R. M. *Moral Thinking: Its Levels, Method, and Point.* Oxford: Oxford University Press, 1981.

Heinaman, Robert. "Rationality, *Eudaimonia* and *Kakodaimonia* in Aristotle." *Phronesis* 38 (1993): 31–56.

———. "*Eudaimonia* and Self-Sufficiency in the *Nicomachean Ethics.*" *Phronesis* 33 (1988): 31–53.

Hossenfelder, Malte. 1986. "Epicurus—Hedonist *malgré lui.*" In *The Norms of Nature: Studies in Hellenistic Ethics.* Ed. Malcolm Schofield and Gisela Striker. Cambridge: Cambridge University Press, 1986.

Hughes, Gerard. *Aristotle on Ethics.* New York: Routledge, 2001.

Hunt, Lester. "Flourishing Egoism." *Social Philosophy & Policy* 16 (1999): 72–95.

Hurka, Thomas. "The Three Faces of Flourishing." *Social Philosophy & Policy* 16 (1999): 44–71.

Hursthouse, Rosalind, Gavin Lawrence, and Warren Quinn, eds. *Virtues and Reasons.* Oxford: Oxford University Press, 1995.

Inwood, Brad. *Ethics and Human Action in Early Stoicism.* Oxford: Oxford University Press, 1985.

Inwood, Brad, and Lloyd Gerson, eds. *Hellenistic Philosophy: Introductory Readings.* Indianapolis: Hackett Publishing Co., 1998.

Irwin, Terence. "Permanent Happiness: Aristotle and Solon." In *Aristotle's Ethics: Critical Essays.* Ed. Nancy Sherman. Lanham, MD: Rowman & Littlefield Publishers, 1999.

―――. "The Virtues: Theory and Common Sense in Greek Philosophy." In *How Should One Live? Essays on the Virtues.* Ed. Roger Crisp. Oxford: Oxford University Press, 1998.

―――. "Ethics in the *Rhetoric* and in the *Ethics.*" In *Essays on Aristotle's Rhetoric.* Ed. Amélie Oksenberg Rorty. Berkeley: University of California Press, 1996.

―――. *Plato's Ethics.* New York: Oxford University Press, 1995.

―――. "Prudence and Morality in Greek Ethics." *Ethics* 105 (1995): 284–95.

―――. "Socrates the Epicurean." In *Essays on the Philosophy of Socrates.* Ed. Hugh Benson. New York: Oxford University Press, 1992.

―――. *Aristotle's First Principles.* Oxford: Oxford University Press, 1988.

―――. "Stoic and Aristotelian Conceptions of Happiness." In *The Norms of Nature: Studies in Hellenistic Ethics.* Ed. Malcolm Schofield and Gisela Striker. Cambridge: Cambridge University Press, 1986.

―――. *Plato's Moral Theory: The Early and Middle Dialogues.* Oxford: Oxford University Press, 1977.

Jonsen, Albert and Stephen Toulmin. *The Abuse of Casuistry: A History of Moral Reasoning.* Berkeley: University of California Press, 1988.

Kahn, Charles. "Plato's Theory of Desire." *Review of Metaphysics* 41 (1987): 77–103.

Kant, Immanuel. *Metaphysics of Morals.* Trans. John Ladd (first pt.) and James Ellington (second pt.). Indianapolis: Hackett Publishing Co., 1999 (first pt.) and 1983 (second pt.).

―――. *Groundwork of the Metaphysics of Morals.* Trans. H. J. Paton. New York: Harper & Row, 1964.

―――. *Critique of Practical Reason.* Trans. Lewis Beck. New York: Macmillan Publishing Company, 1956.

―――. *Fundamental Principles of the Metaphysic of Morals.* Trans. Thomas Abott. Indianapolis: Bobbs-Merrill Company, 1949.

Kenny, Anthony. *Aristotle on the Perfect Life.* Oxford: Oxford University Press, 1992.

Klosko, George. "The Rule of Reason in Plato's Psychology." *History of Philosophy Quarterly* 5 (1988): 341–56.

Kraut, Richard. "Aristotle on the Human Good: An Overview." In *Aristotle's Ethics: Critical Essays*. Ed. Nancy Sherman. Lanham, MD: Rowman & Littlefield Publishers, 1999.

———. *Aristotle on the Human Good*. Princeton, NJ: Princeton University Press, 1989.

Laertius, Diogenes. *Lives of Eminent Philosophers* [DH]. Vol. 2. Loeb Classical Library. Cambridge, MA: Harvard University Press, 1995.

Larmore, Charles. *Patterns of Moral Complexity*. Cambridge: Cambridge University Press, 1987.

Lear, Jonathan. *Happiness, Death, and the Remainder of Life*. Cambridge, MA: Harvard University Press, 2000.

———. *Aristotle and the Desire to Understand*. Cambridge: Cambridge University Press, 1988.

Liddell, Henry, and Robert Scott. *A Greek-English Lexicon*. New York: Oxford University Press, 1985.

Lloyd, A. C. "Emotion and Decision in Stoic Psychology." In *The Stoics*. Ed. J. M. Rist. Berkeley: University of California Press, 1978.

Long, A. A. *Stoic Studies*. Cambridge: Cambridge University Press, 1996.

Long, A. A. and D. N. Sedley. *The Hellenistic Philosophers*. Vol. 1: Greek and Latin Texts. Vol. 2: Translations with Philosophical Commentary. Cambridge: Cambridge University Press, 1987.

Lories, Danielle. *Le Sens Commun et le Jugement du* Phronimos: *Aristote et les Stoïciens*. Louvain-la-Neuve: Editions Peeters, 1998.

MacIntyre, Alasdair. *Whose Justice? Whose Rationality?* Notre Dame, IN: University of Notre Dame Press, 1988.

———. *After Virtue*. 2d ed. Notre Dame, IN: University of Notre Dame Press, 1983.

McDowell, John. "The Role of *Eudaimonia* in Aristotle's Ethics." In *Essays on Aristotle's Ethics*. Ed. Amélie Oksenberg Rorty. Berkeley: University of California Press, 1980.

Mele, Alfred. "Aristotle on the Roles of Reason in Motivation and Judgment." *Archiv für Geschichte der Philosophie* 66 (1983): 124–47.

———. "Choice and Virtue in the *Nicomachean Ethics*." *Journal of the History of Philosophy* 19 (1981): 405–23.

Mill, John Stuart. *Utilitarianism*. Buffalo: Prometheus Books, 1987.

Mitsis, Phillip. *Epicurus' Ethical Theory: The Pleasures of Invulnerability*. New York: Cornell University Press, 1988.

Modrak, Deborah. "Aristotle on Reason, Practical Reason, and Living Well." In *Aristotle's Ethics*. Ed. John Anton and Anthony Preus. Albany, State University of New York Press, 1991.

Murdoch, Iris. "The Sovereignty of Good over Other Concepts." In *Virtue Ethics*. Ed. Roger Crisp and Michael Slote. Oxford: Oxford University Press, 1997.

———. *The Sovereignty of the Good*. Boston: Routledge & Kegan Paul, 1970.

Nagel, Thomas. "Aristotle on *Eudaimonia*." In *Essays on Aristotle's Ethics*. Ed. Amélie Oksenberg Rorty. Berkeley: University of California Press, 1980.

———. *The Possibility of Altruism*. Oxford: Oxford University Press, 1970.

Natali, Carlo. *The Wisdom of Aristotle*. Trans. Gerald Parks. Albany: State University of New York Press, 2001.

Nehamas, Alexander. "Socratic Intellectualism." In *Proceedings of the Boston Area Colloquium in Ancient Philosophy*. Vol. 2. Ed. John Cleary. Lanham, MD: University Press of America, 1987.

Nelson, Daniel. *The Priority of Prudence: Virtue and Natural Law in Thomas Aquinas and the Implications for Modern Ethics*. University Park: Pennsylvania State University Press, 1992.

Noddings, Nel. *Caring: A Feminine Approach to Ethics and Moral Education*. Berkeley: University of California Press, 1984.

Nussbaum, Martha. "The Discernment of Perception: An Aristotelian Conception of Private and Public Rationality." In *Aristotle's Ethics: Critical Essays*. Ed. Nancy Sherman. Lanham, MD: Rowman & Littlefield Publishers, 1999.

———. *The Fragility of Goodness: Luck and Ethics in Greek Tragedy and Philosophy*. Cambridge: Cambridge University Press. 1986.

Parfit, Derek. *Reasons and Persons*. Oxford: Oxford University Press, 1984.

Paul, Ellen, Fred Miller, and Jeffrey Paul, eds. *Virtue and Vice*. Cambridge: Cambridge University Press, 1998.

———, eds. *Self-Interest*. Cambridge: Cambridge University Press, 1997.

Penner, Terry. "The Unity of Virtue." *Philosophical Review* 82 (1973): 35–68.

Peters, F. E. *Greek Philosophical Terms: A Historical Lexicon*. New York: New York University Press, 1967.

Plato. *Nichomachean Ethics* [NE]. Trans. Christopher Rowe, philosophical introduction and commentary by Sarah Broadie. New York: Oxford University Press, 2002.

———. *Republic* [Rep.]. Loeb Classical Library. Cambridge, MA: Harvard University Press, 1994.

———. *Laches, Protagoras* [Prot.], *Meno* [Meno], *Euthydemus* [Euthyd.]. Loeb Classical Library. Cambridge, MA: Harvard University Press, 1990.

————. *Laws* [*Laws*]. Loeb Classical Library. Cambridge, MA: Harvard University Press, 1984.

————. *Euthyphro* [*Eu.*], *Apology* [*Apol.*], *Crito* [*Crit.*], *Phaedo* [*Phaed.*], *Phaedrus* [*Phdr.*]. Loeb Classical Library. Cambridge, MA: Harvard University Press, 1982.

————. *Statesman* [*St.*], *Philebus* [*Phil.*]. Loeb Classical Library. Cambridge, MA: Harvard University Press, 1975.

Plutarch. *Moralia*. Vol. 6. Loeb Classical Library. Cambridge, MA: Harvard University Press, 1993.

————. *Moralia*. Vol. 13. Loeb Classical Library. Cambridge, MA: Harvard University Press, 1976.

Pomeroy, Sarah, Stanley Burstein, Walter Donlan, and Jennifer Roberts, eds. *Ancient Greece: A Political, Social, and Cultural History*. Oxford: Oxford University Press, 1998.

Posner, Richard. *The Problematics of Moral and Legal Theory*. Cambridge, MA: Harvard University Press, 1999.

Rawls, John. *Lectures in the History of Modern Philosophy*. Cambridge, MA: Harvard University Press, 2000.

————. *A Theory of Justice*. Cambridge, MA: Harvard University Press, 1971.

Reeve, C. D. C. *Practices of Reason: Aristotle's Nicomachean Ethics*. Oxford: Oxford University Press, 1995.

Rist, J. M. "An Early Dispute about Right Reason." *Monist* 66 (1983): 39–48.

————, ed. *The Stoics*. Berkeley: University of California Press, 1978.

Rorty, Amélie Oksenberg, ed. *Essays on Aristotle's* Rhetoric. Berkeley: University of California Press, 1996.

————. *Essays on Aristotle's Ethics*. Berkeley: University of California Press, 1980.

Ross, W. D. *The Right and the Good*. Indianapolis: Hackett Publishing Company, 1988.

Salkever, Stephen. *Finding the Mean*. Princeton, NJ: Princeton University Press, 1990.

Santas, Gerasimos. "Socrates at Work on Virtue and Knowledge." In *The Philosophy of Socrates: A Collection of Critical Essays*. Ed. Gregory Vlastos. New York: Garden City, 1971.

Schaeffer, H. J. *"Phronesis" bei Platon*. Bochum: Brockmeyer, 1981.

Schneewind, J. B. *The Invention of Autonomy*. Cambridge: Cambridge University Press, 1998.

Schofield, Malcolm, and Gisela Striker, eds. *The Norms of Nature: Studies in Hellenistic Ethics*. Cambridge: Cambridge University Press, 1986.

Sherman, Nancy, ed. *Aristotle's Ethics: Critical Essays*. Lanham, MD: Rowman & Littlefield Publishers, 1999.

———. "The Habituation of Character." In *Aristotle's Ethics: Critical Essays*. Ed. Nancy Sherman. Lanham, MD: Rowman & Littlefield Publishers, 1999.

———. *Making a Necessity of Virtue: Aristotle and Kant on Virtue*. Cambridge: Cambridge University Press, 1997.

———. *The Fabric of Character: Aristotle's Theory of Virtue*. Oxford: Oxford University Press, 1989.

Singer, Peter. *Practical Ethics*. Cambridge: Cambridge University Press, 1979.

Smith, A. D. "Character and Intellect in Aristotle's Ethics." *Phronesis* 41 (1995): 56-74.

Smith, Tara. "The Practice of Pride." In *Virtue and Vice*. Ed. Ellen Paul, Fred Miller, and Jeffrey Paul. Cambridge: Cambridge University Press, 1998.

Sorabji, Richard. "Aristotle on the Role of Intellect in Virtue." In *Essays on Aristotle's Ethics*. Ed. Amélie Oksenberg Rorty. Berkeley: University of California Press, 1980.

Stocker, Michael. "The Schizophrenia of Modern Ethical Theories." *Journal of Philosophy* 73 (1976): 453–56.

Stout, Jeffrey. *Ethics after Babel*. Boston: Beacon Press, 1988.

Tessitore, Aristide. *Reading Aristotle's Ethics: Virtue, Rhetoric, and Political Philosophy*. Albany: State University of New York Press, 1996.

Thompson, Michael. "The Representation of Life." In *Virtues and Reasons*. Ed. Rosalind Hursthouse, Gavin Lawrence, and Warren Quinn. Oxford: Oxford University Press, 1995.

Tuozzo, Thomas. "Aristotelian Deliberation Is Not of Ends." In *Aristotle's Ethics*. Ed. John Anton and Anthony Preus. Albany: State University Press of New York, 1991.

Urmson, J. O. *Aristotle's Ethics*. Oxford: Basil Blackwell, 1988.

Vlastos, Gregory. *Socrates, Ironist and Moral Philosopher*. Ithaca, NY: Cornell University Press, 1991.

———. *Platonic Studies*, 2d ed. Princeton, NJ: Princeton University Press, 1981.

———. "The Unity of the Virtues in the *Protagoras*." In *Platonic Studies*, 2d ed. Princeton, NJ: Princeton University Press, 1981.

———, ed. *The Philosophy of Socrates: A Collection of Critical Essays*. New York: Garden City, 1971.

White, Stephen. *Sovereign Virtue: Aristotle on the Relation between Happiness and Prosperity*. Stanford: Stanford University Press, 1992.

Wiggins, David. "Deliberation and Practical Reasoning." In *Essays on Aristotle's Ethics*. Ed. Amélie Oksenberg Rorty. Berkeley: University of California Press, 1980.

Williams, Bernard. *Ethics and the Limits of Philosophy*. Cambridge, MA: Harvard University Press, 1985.

Xenophon. *Memorabilia* [*Memo.*]. Loeb Classical Library. Cambridge, MA: Harvard University Press, 1987.

Zagzebski, Linda Trinkhaus. *Virtues of the Mind: An Inquiry into the Nature of Virtue and the Ethical Foundations of Knowledge*. Cambridge: Cambridge University Press, 1996.

Index

Note: The location of the primary entry about a topic or philosopher is indicated with **bold** page numbers.